I'm Becoming What I'm Becoming

Jewish Perspectives

by

Rabbi Benjamin Edidin Scolnic

2008
Russell Enterprises, Inc.
Milford, CT USA

I'm Becoming What I'm Becoming

Jewish Perspectives

ISBN: 978-1-888690-54-5

Published by:
Russell Enterprises, Inc.
P.O. Box 5460
Milford, CT 06460 USA

http://www.chesscafe.com
info@chesscafe.com

Rabbi Scolnic can be contacted by email at rabbi.scolnic@gmail.com.

Cover design by Janel Lowrance.
Photograph of stained glass window in the sanctuary of Temple Beth Sholom in Hamden, Connecticut by Hank Paper.
Back cover photo by David Ottenstein.

Printed in the United States of America

Table of Contents

Introduction

Recently, I was asked to give a speech about my favorite verses in the Bible. At first, I declined the invitation, claiming that I couldn't reduce my love of the Bible to a few selected verses. When pressed, however, I found to my surprise that it was easy to arrive at my favorite verse of all. The scene is that commonly referred to as "the Burning Bush" in which God speaks to Moses on Mt. Sinai and calls him to lead the people out of slavery in Egypt. Moses asks for God's Name. The real answer is that God does not have a name, because a name is a definition and God is infinite. So God states a name that is not a name at all: "I am Becoming what I am Becoming." You may have heard the translation "I am that I am," but that is imprecise and indicates that God is Who He is, a static entity. On the contrary, God is dynamic and responsive to the evolving needs of humanity.

When God commands Moses to return to Egypt and liberate the Israelite slaves, Moses doesn't want to accept the role, claiming that he's not a speaker. It may not be literally true, but many traditions explain that he stutters. If Moses does have a speech impediment and has to rely on his brother Aaron as his spokesman for a while, he soon grows beyond his disability and his reliance on others and speaks eloquently and at great length over the course of his lifetime.

In other words, when God says that He is Becoming, He also indicates that Moses is in a process of change that will enable him to carry out on of the greatest moral missions of all time. And God is telling us something important about our lives, that we don't understand the importance of becoming. How many of us say, "I am what I am," claiming that we cannot change our ways even if we want to. This is nonsense: we can be more than we've been.

And yet it's true that, in a sense, we are all stutterers, reluctant to take on the tasks with which life has presented us. We all need some help. We need God's guidance and we need an Aaron by our side, a spouse, a brother or sister, a special friend, someone to support us when we're afraid to become who we're supposed to be.

The cover of this book is an artist's depiction of the Burning Bush scene. It is a photograph of a stained glass window in the sanctuary of Temple Beth Sholom in Hamden, Connecticut, a synagogue that I've had the honor to serve for twenty-five years.

This is my fourth book of thoughts about the changes that we need to make in order to fulfill ourselves as human beings. We need to draw on our memories and our hopes, our sense of the past and our visions of the future. We must be concerned about the natural environment and the issues that divide our country and our world and nourish our minds, our bodies and our spirits so that we can act on those concerns.

None of us is Moses, and we're not called upon to liberate a nation of slaves, but each of us is alive for a reason, and we have to find out what that is, and live accordingly.

Rabbi Benjamin Edidin Scolnic
Hamden, Connecticut
July 2008

Chapter One

Bubbi Doesn't Know Who She Is,
But You Know Who You Are

A man who has always been a smart dresser wears a tie that doesn't match his suit.

A woman who would never go outside without her hair done and her face looking just right walks into a store without make-up.

An aunt who was always fastidious about financial matters sends you a birthday check written in pencil.

Little things: nothing important, but signs that the person is losing his or her identity.

It's horrible for the people, when they see the rest of their lives as a tunnel that is getting darker and darker.

And it's horrible for their loved ones: for the spouses who try to compensate for each other so that the kids won't make them move; for the kids who would do anything but are powerless to stop the process.

Many of us have lived through this; we grieved for the people we loved long before they passed away. As they lost their identities, day by day, piece by piece, we grieved, as if they were dying over and over again.

The lady my kids call Bubbi New York has lived at our house for a number of years now, and so my family has watched it all happen. We've lived the process with her and for the last few years, without her. For some time now, she hasn't known who she is, or who anyone else is. There's nothing else wrong with her physically; in fact, she's doing very well in every other respect. She does like to eat, and now she even eats pizza, something she never ate before, because she doesn't remember that she hates cheese.

As I watched helplessly as the process unfolded, I noticed that there were a few things that were so at the core of her identity that they would emerge for a moment from somewhere deep in her consciousness. She loves babies; someplace deep inside her is the maternal instinct that was operative in her life. She still hates *schmutz*; she'll take five minutes to search and destroy pieces of lint on my kids' clothes. And she remembers pieces of some of the most famous Jewish songs and prayers: *Kol Nidre, Dayyenu, Mah Nishtana, Had Gadya*, the *Motzi*. Someplace, deep down at her core, is Judaism.

When she used to tell me about her childhood in Munich, Germany, in the 1930s, she would describe walking to *shul* with her parents and sisters, holding her father's hand, as Nazis jeered at them and insulted them.

But she was Jewish:
when she was put on a train that went to Poland but then came back;
when she and one of her sisters won the lottery of the *Kindertransport* to escape to freedom in England;
when she eventually found out that her parents were alive and well after being hid in a monastery in Italy;
when she came to America and married a Polish Jewish man who had survived Auschwitz;
when she lived to see her six grandchildren have a Bar or Bat Mitzvah ceremony and a granddaughter married under a *chuppa*.

And now she sees a Jewish great-grandchild, even though to her it's just a baby, like one of her dolls.

So the disease has stolen her identity, but there's still something left, and most of that identity is Jewish.

At one point a couple of years ago we discovered something that added insult to the injury. A criminal had stolen her identity and was writing checks using her name. It boggled my mind; it was as if an insidious disease and an insidious person merged to steal her name.

I was forced to learn about identity theft. I learned that in 2003, 5% of adults in this country suffered from identity theft of some kind. Since 2003 it's gone down to around 4%, because people have learned how to monitor this sphere of their lives better. A lot of us have learned that there are things that we can do to prevent identity theft. Ironically, cyber-savvy young people are less likely to take basic precautions to prevent the theft of their identities.

So I think about Bubbi, victim of double identity-theft. Every time she says or sings a word of a prayer or a song, I am grateful that there's a little of her left. You get to a point where you are grateful for hints, the tiniest clues that she's still there.

Identity is a vague term. Jewish identity means different things to different people. That's fine; we can be Jewish in different ways.

What I'm asking is: What does Jewish identity mean to you? It obviously means something or you wouldn't be reading this.

Still, many of us would have trouble answering the question. We would be hard-pressed to articulate what our Jewishness means to us.

- We can't remember our mother's Hebrew name.
- We can't remember how to say the blessings when called to the Torah.
- We can't remember what the holiday a few days after Yom Kippur is called.

Little things, you think, nothing so crucial; but signs that we are losing our Jewish identities.

No disease took our Jewish identities away.

No criminal took our Jewish identities away.

But just as in criminal identity theft, many of us do not do what we need to, basic things, to prevent the loss of our Jewish identities.

And just as in criminal identity theft, it is our young people, otherwise so savvy about so many things, who don't realize how likely they are to lose their identities.

Let's be very basic and talk about what Jewishness means. We have to differentiate between two aspects of Jewishness.

First, it means to be a member of the Jewish people.

Second, Jewishness also can mean adhering to the faith and observing the practices of the religion called Judaism.

Jewish people do not necessarily identify with both of these aspects of Jewishness. I know many, many people who are legally Jewish, identify as Jewish, but care not a bit about Judaism, its beliefs or practices.

Daniel Pearl was such a person. Some of us saw the movie *A Mighty Heart* about the abduction and murder of the *Wall Street Journal* reporter Daniel Pearl. Pearl was murdered in Karachi, Pakistan on February 21st, 2002. His tormentors defined Daniel Pearl as Jewish. Why did the Muslim thugs kill Daniel Pearl? He wasn't religious. It had nothing to do with his practice of Judaism. But Pearl agreed with their definition of his identity. His final words were "I am Jewish." He rose above the hopelessness of his situation with incredible courage and asserted his identity in the bravest way imaginable. In the end, just as at the end of a life of a person who has dementia, his Jewishness was at his core. He freely claimed his link in the chain of his family and his people. He connected himself with that long list, that horribly long list of Jewish people over the course of history who lost their lives simply because they were Jewish.

After Daniel Pearl was executed, his father, Judea Pearl, edited a book called *I Am Jewish*. Various famous Jewish figures wrote essays about the meaning of Jewishness. They point out that we have the choice whether to be Jewish or not. If you are born Jewish you can say that one or both of your parents were Jewish but you can ignore your roots and be whatever you want.

And yet, your Jewishness is at the core of your identity.

We usually think about our obligations to others. I am not thinking here about your obligations to anyone else, not even your loved ones or your community. I am speaking about your obligations to yourself, to the inner you, to your core identity.

You know your identity, but what are you actually doing to *identify* yourself as Jewish, to promote and nourish what is at your core?

I can't speak for anyone else in this world but I can speak for myself. So let me tell you about my core, why I'm Jewish. I'm not just Jewish because I was born that way.

I am Jewish[1] because wherever and whenever there is suffering, the Jewish person cries. We do not just weep for other Jewish people; we weep for every human being who suffers, from the hungry child in New Haven to the victim of rape in the Sudan to the oppressed women throughout the world to the victims of brutal and senseless murder at Virginia Tech or in Cheshire, Connecticut or the victims of negligence in New Orleans or a bridge in Minnesota. My Jewishness, from my very core, demands that I care about everyone, that I am not just so wrapped up in my little comfortable world that I can ignore and dismiss the horrors that happen all the time in our world.

I am Jewish because I believe that the Jewish people have a destiny to promote morality and peace in this immoral and violent world. My Jewishness will not let me stay quiet in the face of injustice.

A year and a half after Hurricane Katrina, I went to New Orleans with a group of rabbis and helped to clear out rooms that, due to the ineptness and negli-

---

[1] The idea here is based on *Why I Am a Jew* by Edmond Fleg (1927).

gence of the local government, were still in disarray. And in the afternoon we stopped and gathered in a classroom and *davened mincha*, we sang the afternoon service, and the kids of that inner city school watched and gawked in amazement. But I was never so proud to be Jewish as when I stood there as a rabbi covered with dust and sang the *kaddish*, the prayer in which we express our yearnings for a better world. You have to get your hands dirty in this world if you're going to help clean it up.

I'm sure that your Jewishness calls to you in the same way. You can't just cry about the suffering of others.

I am Jewish because Judaism does not mean that I have to leave my brain at the door. I don't have to dismiss scientific evidence in order to preserve the truth of my faith. Judaism teaches me to use my mind and use it well. And Judaism itself evolves, as we learn more and more of God's truth.

And so I am Jewish because I believe that all human beings, males and females, are created in the image of God. I reject any religion or any movement of any religion that raises males over females in any way.

And we continue to grow, understanding more about what makes people tick. And as we learn more, Judaism will change, because we do not believe in prejudice of any kind and we must acknowledge our lack of knowledge when we learn more.

I am Jewish because, as in the message of the High Holidays, we acknowledge that we are not perfect and that we can make up for our mistakes and that there are second chances.

I am Jewish because, as in the message of the holiday of *Tu B'Shvat*, I believe that the earth is the Lord's and that human beings must not destroy it out of greed.

I am Jewish and I support the State of Israel in its courageous fight of self-defense. You will nod in agreement. But what exactly do you do for Israel? I know that you watch the news and in the privacy of your own den rooted for Israel. But I mean, what do you concretely do for Israel?

Those of us who have traveled to Israel recently can say:
I showed my support by being there. While the rest of the world scorns Israel, I was there.
I asserted my identity as a Jewish person by walking in the footsteps of my ancestors.
I was touched by the spirituality of the Holy Land.

I saw the fulfillment of the promise of the Promised Land.

For those who go to Israel who have never been there before, it is a way of fulfilling a personal dream of a lifetime. For those who go for a second or a tenth time, it can be life changing in what it means for our Jewishness.

Any trip to Israel is an unmistakable assertion of identity.

If you've never been to Israel, and you can physically and financially afford to go, you must go at least once in your life. If you haven't been there in a long time, you wouldn't recognize the place. It's beautiful and prosperous and green and vibrant. Don't let the negative propaganda fool you. It's the center of the world.

I want to say something to all of our young people. You cannot imagine what it means to your parents and grandparents when you act on your Jewishness. We take nothing for granted. We never assume anything. I know that when I see my youngest child, my Sarah, active in her youth group, bringing other kids into Judaism, I'm happy in ways that I can't express. You'd think: Well, sure, Rabbi's daughter, Jewish day school education; of course she's active. But that's not how I see it. I see Jewishness in my family going on in the next generation, and I feel gratified in my core. Sarah sits every evening next to her Bubbi on the couch in the den. Bubbi is staring blankly at the television. Sarah is multi-tasking: Doing her homework, watching television, and IM-ing and texting her youth group members. I feel that Bubbi's identity has gone into her granddaughter, and I feel comfort. So to use the language of the younger generation, I want to give a "shout out" to every young person who cares about his or her Judaism: Thank you for being true to your family and to yourself.

Let me explain what I mean by being true to yourself. Over twenty years ago, I wrote a doctoral thesis about Biblical lists, all of the boring passages in the Bible. It was a perfect topic for me: I'm a very boring person and found the topic very exciting. But then my life started and I had a job and kids and I was busy and it took years for me just to make a few changes so that it could be published. When I sent it in for publication, I noticed that the end of the book was really the beginning of the next book. There was an idea there, a really profound idea, better than my thesis, and I said at the end of the first book that I'd soon be writing the second one. And guess what? I've never written that book with that great idea. I have terrific excuses, and I've written other books, but somehow, I've never done that one that is so close to my heart. The pub-lisher waited, year after year, for me to fulfill my contract, but then things were getting pressing. So last year, after Yom Kippur, I sat down to start typ-ing, and you know what? I no longer had a real grasp of my own idea. So I decided to get into it by writing the first chapter that is on a text in an ancient language you've never heard of called Ugaritic. Only a few people in the world know Ugaritic, but in my day, I was great at Ugaritic: I could read it and translate it at sight. But now, I could only recognize some letters; I no longer had the tools to write that chapter. That's what happens: Use it or lose it.

But if I would try, I could get the Ugaritic back. I have to do it. If I don't write that book, no one else in the whole world will care. But I'll care, not just because it's a really good idea, but because it's an expression of who I am, down in my core, where ideas matter. To leave that book unwritten would be a sin against myself. I have to be true to myself. I have to fulfill who I am.

For many Jewish people, Hebrew has become Ugaritic. At your Bar Mitzvah ceremony, the rabbi said that you were the greatest thing since Wheaties. Now, you can sing along with the familiar and famous songs, *Kol Nidre*, *Adon Olam*, but that's about it. You have the general idea, but you can't articulate it or express it. It's as if you've retreated into dementia like Bubbi, with your Jewishness only re-awakening for moments at a time.

But if you tried, you could get your Hebrew back. It takes some patience and time and energy. But you could get it back. And you could retrieve part of yourself, a part that you've forgotten.

So I've sketched some of the reasons I'm Jewish, the reasons I am who I am, the bases of my identity.

Identity is one thing; identification, the ways by which we express our identity, is something else. But none of this is so hard. Identification is done by doing easy things, going to a service, reading a Jewish book or taking a class.

I keep thinking about all those movies where an official demands: "Stop and identify yourself."

And I keep thinking about Bubbi, who can't identify herself, who has no idea who she is, but somehow, down at the core of what's left, in the fragments and the pieces of memories, still is what she is, and that's a Jewish person.

For everything that she's lost, she still is what she is.

I hope that none of us lose our identities the way that Bubbi has.

It's true she's not suffering, and so many of us go through such unspeakable suffering and pain. But how horrible not to be yourself any more.

First a disease and then a criminal stole her identity.

But nothing and no one has stolen your identity.
You've just let it evaporate into the air.

You've been like me, not writing the book that means so much to you, not keeping the contract you signed. You have a contract, a sacred covenant, with God, with your ancestors, and with yourself. You've been putting it off, year after year. Nobody will care if I write that book. But a lot of people will care if you assert your Jewishness.

Remember your obligations to yourself.
You have your memories;
you have your knowledge;
you know who you are.
You have an identity.
Please stop and identify yourself.

Chapter Two

Why Am I Soft in the Middle (when) the Rest of My Life Is So Hard?

So here I am in Israel, at a Karaoke pub inside a hotel, drinking my Pepsi Max, standing outside the window, looking in because I can't stand all of the cigarette smoke. And these beautiful Israeli kids are having a blast, singing all of the hit songs. I know a lot of prayers in Hebrew and a lot of traditional Hebrew songs but I don't know any of these Israeli hits. All of the kids know all of the words to all of the songs, and they're singing with each sacrificial lamb that dares to go up to the microphone. Kids having a good time, singing and smoking and drinking.

So why do I keep standing there, riveted? I can't go anywhere, and I don't know why. It's not my scene. I don't smoke and I don't drink. And I don't know the songs and I can't sing anyway. I realize eventually that there's something about these young people that is drawing my attention. I talk to one of them, a young man named Eitan. He tells me that he's been in the army for a couple of years. He's twenty years old. Like every Israeli teenager, he went into the army at eighteen years old. He doesn't like being in the army; it's rigorous training and hard conditions and lousy pay. And in the summer he was in Lebanon fighting against Hezbollah. And when he says the word Hezbollah, referring to the enemy who has sworn to destroy Israel, his voice does not change; he does not speak with spite or anger. And yet, there is something that I can feel, and it's his strength, his toughness; his resolve. But now it's his turn to sing and he goes back to being a kid. And he sings a song about love. And he does so well that the crowd calls for an encore.

But he refuses, playfully, and instead a young woman, who obviously knows him, starts singing a song about a *Yeled Rah* or "Bad Boy". And she points her finger at Eitan and he just loves it, and so does everybody else.

Eventually, Eitan is nice enough to come over to me again, and he says that one of his friends told him that I am a rabbi from America. I asked him what he's going to do. And now I hear another voice, and he talks about finishing his military service, taking a year to travel, and then studying biomedical engineering, working on devices to help people. He decided to go into the field after seeing some terrible things happen to his buddies in the army.

So I had the picture: A bad boy, a rascal, who had gone into the army and now knows what he wants to do with his life.

Why Am I Soft in the Middle (when) the Rest of My Life Is So Hard?

And then I thought about all of the young people I know in America, some of whom have direction, but at least as many who *never* have a real direction, who fall into a job or spend many years figuring themselves out.

And I wondered if America doesn't need a program through which all young people should have to do some kind of national service after high school, whether the high school-straight-into-college route does not simply prolong adolescence and dependence on parents.

Purpose in life is something that *can* be promoted. I believe that every person in this world is in this world for at least one reason. The challenge in life is to find your purpose. God created this world for a reason and He created *you* for a reason.

If you believe this, your sense of yourself will completely change. I talked to a group in a teen class some years ago and told them that their job was to discover their purpose. After the class left, one girl came back into my office and asked me what her purpose was. I said that I could guess but that it was her job to find out. The good news is that it took four years but she discovered it, and her life is on a constructive track.

Too many of our young people are not on track. I was talking to a young man. I'm very fond of him. His name is Scott and he's on my archaeological dig in the Sinai desert. He's bright, good-looking, and a genuinely good and kind soul. But he has no purpose in life. He's worked on a Ph.D. for years but he's sick of his thesis and doesn't want to finish it. He's been in a relationship for four years with a wonderful girl but he doesn't want to risk commitment.

And I say to him, "Your problem is that you live for yourself. Purpose is outer-directed, and *you* are completely inner-directed." He looks at me in complete bewilderment. And I wonder if Scott, and all the young people he represents, would not have benefited from service to his community or his country at a younger age, something that would have moved him out of himself so that he could have found out who he's supposed to be.

I run into a girl in Israel. She's American and she's now been to Israel eight times at the age of 30. I ask her if she's volunteered or participated in programs. "No," she says, "I keep going to Israel to find myself." And I say, "Israel's a small country. Maybe you're looking for yourself in all the wrong places. You're not really living in Israel; you're using Israel as a fantasy vacationland. A vacation by definition is a respite from reality. You need to find out your purpose in the real world." *She* looks at me in complete bewilderment.

She doesn't get what my Israeli friend Eitan gets because Eitan, the bad boy, served his country and emerged from the experience as a man who cares about others. He has purpose and he has what I call "emotional *abs*."

You know what *abs* are, the muscles in the *ab*domen, the stomach. Think about Rocky and all physically-fit people, working on their abs. You can punch them in the stomach and they'll be fine. They may wince, they may stagger backwards, but then they stand up straight and tall again.

I'm telling you that we Americans today are soft in the middle.

We are soft in the middle because we indulge ourselves.

We want to eat what we want to eat. If we don't feel like exercising or just walking for a few months at a time, we make up wonderful excuses, how it's cold outside or our knees hurt or the gym's too expensive or our favorite, we're "just too busy."

How expensive is it to give up what could have been extra years of life because of our laziness?

How busy could we be that we couldn't use some extra years that a decent diet and some regular exercise might just buy us?

But NOOO, we need our *chazarai*. I'm not even talking about the real *chazarai* that many of us eat; don't even get me started on that. I mean the junk and the trash and the garbage we happily consume in the name of indulgence.

We Americans today are soft in the middle; we can't resist anything. Since we lack discipline, we don't have emotional abs. We cannot take a punch. When life hits us, we are knocked down for the count of ten.

We read the story of Abraham and Isaac and we are horrified. How could Abraham have been willing to sacrifice the child for whom he'd waited one hundred years?

But we American parents are at the opposite extreme: We coddle ourselves and we live to coddle our children. We want to shield them from all harm and in the process we forget to teach them how to deal with harm when it comes.

In Judaism, every parent must teach their child how to swim, which of course is a metaphor. But we're so desperate to keep our children away from the deep end that we never take them to the pool at all, and then when life throws them in anyway, they don't know what to do.

We have to teach them how to take a punch.

In the recent movie, *Rocky Balboa*, the aging ex-champion tells his son: It's not how hard you hit. It's how you take the hits and keep moving forward. Life will hit you hard.

We have to help our children develop emotional and mental abs.
We have to show them the world, and not just from a hotel window.
We have to show them what poverty and sickness and homelessness are.
We have to teach them about hunger and thirst.
We have to teach them about dealing with anxiety and rejection.
We have to show them about the infirmities of old age.
We have to teach them about death and grief and mourning.

When my first child, my Rachel, was three, I decided that I would never discuss death in the house. If I officiated at a funeral, I said I was doing a service. If someone died, I didn't mention it. And when her goldfish died I ran to get another one. She couldn't understand how the goldfish doubled in size in an hour. I said it was pregnant. She asked how it got pregnant. That's when I really started sweating. Before I could answer, we heard a scream. We ran outside and the man across the street had died and was being taken out of the house on a stretcher. I realized then and there that I could not shield Rachel from death. And then when a beautiful little boy in her nursery school class died the next year, I knew it once and for all: There is no shielding; there is no protecting. Better to teach your child well, and completely, about life. A new goldfish won't work. Don't teach them things they'll have to *unlearn*.

Exercise their emotional abs, their mental abs, their spiritual abs.

Why don't we do this? We're trying to protect them because we love them so much. But our loving and caring approach raises weak and spoiled and dependent children who have trouble becoming adults.

Why do we do this? Because we're scared for them. And why are we scared for them? Because *we're* so scared of life.

It's so ironic; we have it so good and we feel so bad.

We had unreal expectations of life; that life would give us inside straights, straight A's, no traffic jams, and a partridge in a pear tree, whatever that means.

And we're anxious, terrified, panicked, stressed and overwhelmed.

You're not an Israeli parent who has to send your child into the army, but you're at least as afraid.

And even though you know better, you tell them to expect straight A's, inside straights, no traffic jams and a partridge in a pear tree.

And when they have to fold with a bad hand or fail an exam or hit traffic or buy a house with an empty pear tree, they don't know what to do, because you taught them to expect only the best.

And they become anxious, panicked, stressed and overwhelmed.
And they become afraid.
Fear is the heritage we transmit to the new generation.

People talk to me who are shocked, shocked that they have gotten sick or that they have suffered a loss or that they have a problem of any kind.
"I was never sick before."
"I never lost anyone so close to me."
"I never expected to have a problem like this!"
At the moment, feeling for their suffering, I express compassion.

But when I step back from what they're feeling, I want to say, "Are you kidding? Why are you shocked?"

You're going to get punched.
Anyone, including your loving parents, who told you differently, was painting a fairy tale.
You must live expecting to get punched and train yourself and prepare yourself to take the punch.

I don't know what Judaism means to you.
But I think that among other things, Judaism is an abs machine for the emotions and the spirit.
Judaism says: "Just do it."

When you pray three times a day, there are plenty of times that you don't feel like praying. You do it anyway. You become disciplined.

You go to a restaurant and you can only eat one or two things on the menu: You learn to be disciplined so that when the doctor tells you to stop eating certain things you just stop eating those things.

Why Am I Soft in the Middle (when) the Rest of My Life Is So Hard?

When you're part of a community and not just in your own little fantasy bubble, you see people lose their loved ones and you see people get sick and you see every problem under the sun and you realize that you are no more immune to such things than they are.

You prepare yourself to take a punch.
Judaism is an abs machine, preparing your stomach to take a hit.
It makes you stronger right where it counts.

I'm talking here about two things, our lack of purpose and our weakness.
What's the connection?
Our weakness messes us up and makes us self-indulgent; we're so focused on ourselves that we have no other purpose.

And I think about Eitan, who conquered fear, transcended self-indulgence and emerged not broken but whole, not driven by personal needs but the needs of others.

The name Eitan comes from the Hebrew root Natan, "to give." Eitan means, "I will give." There's a Hebrew phrase, three short Hebrew words, I've always loved: *teyn li koach*. The word *teyn* comes from the same root *natan*.

When I was a supercilious kid in Hebrew School, driving my teachers crazy, they would point to a sign put up on the wall because of my antics. It said *teyn li koach*: "Give me strength."

Now, as an adult, it's what I ask God for.
We all pray for different things and different people.

But my special prayer for you and me is the three words my poor Hebrew School teachers said like a mantra at the time of their great travail, when they had to try to teach the *yeled ra* of the song at the Israeli disco, the bad little boy who was the rabbi's son and had to be treated carefully: *teyn li koach*. "Give me strength."

Give me the strength, give me the abs to do sit ups when I want to lie down flat on the mat and not get up.

Teyn li koach to stand up to those who treat me badly.
Give me strength to take care of the people around me.
Give me strength to take care of myself.

That's one prayer.

My other prayer is that each of us finds the purpose of our lives.

It may be caring for another person.
It may be a job that needs to be done.
It may be participating in community matters.
It may be supporting another person who is doing important things.
But that purpose has to be something besides yourself.
You are not the beginning and end of the world.
You must give.

Paul Simon sang:
> *Why am I soft in the middle*
> *The rest of my life is so hard?*

I would answer the question like this:
Life *is* hard, but we make it even harder by being soft in the middle.

God doesn't want us weak and dependent on Him, abdicating our responsibilities to others and ourselves.

So work on your abs.
Work on your physical strength.
Work on being strong enough not to give a punch but to take a punch and stay upright.

You will get sick here and there. When you get to a certain age, if it's not this it will be that. Sometimes, we should be grateful it's *this* and not *that*.

And work on your emotional strength.
Don't cave in every time you get hit.
Don't be so sensitive to every remark every insensitive person says to you.
Don't let other people define who you are.
Get some abs.
And to the young people who don't know who they are, I beg you:
Don't just look for a job: Look for a purpose.
Look for what you want to do, not just to make a living, but so that you will be living with meaning.

And so I say my other prayer:

> *Adonai oz le-ammo **yeteyn***
> *Adonai yevarech le-ammo bashalom*

Why Am I Soft in the Middle (when) the Rest of My Life Is So Hard?

May God give us strength, because by giving us strength, He'll give us shalom, completeness and purpose. If we work on ourselves, God will be with us, giving us the strength to give.

Chapter Three

Help! or Are You a Scorekeeper?

So I'm fifteen years old and I'm in the car with my father and I'm blaring mad. I can still feel it: We're on Greentree Road in Bethesda, Maryland and my father is driving me against my will to get a haircut. It's 1968 and I don't want a haircut. The Beatles are playing on the radio, singing the song "Help!" My father shuts off the radio, claiming that all this long hair nonsense began with those Beach Boys and so it was their fault to begin with.

I'm very upset. How can I survive at Walt Whitman Senior High School if I get a haircut? Long hair is in and I desperately want to be in. I try my best card, saying to him, "How will I have a chance with Linda Sternfeld if I get a haircut?" But he doesn't hear me. And I can still hear my father saying, "I don't care if you like me. I don't want anything back from you. I'm raising you the best way I know how. And when, someday, God willing, you'll have children, you'll pay me back by raising them the best way you know how. That's the way it works; I take care of you and you'll take care of them. I'm not expecting one thing back from you except that you'll take care of the next generation."

My father said words like these many times over the years. I only remember that particular lecture because the ending was so traumatic. He stood there next to me at Mr. Kaiser's Barber Shop and kept saying, "Take more off! Take more off!" At that moment, my father could be certain that I would not be eager to do anything good for him, so it was just as well that he wasn't expecting anything back from me.

My father raised me with the concept that parents do for their children and their children need not do anything back for their parents. But, as you know, the years go by and things change. It took me a very long time to realize that my father might have believed the "I do for you, you do for your children" philosophy then, when he was in his forties and he was going to live forever in total independence. Now, God bless him, he's twice as old as he was then, and he does have needs, and he needs his children to help. I bought the package he sold me; I thought that I could pay him back by giving to my children. How naive and mistaken I was to think that.

We live in this wonderful time when so many of us live longer in relatively good health. But for all of the wonders of cholesterol drugs and chemotherapy and cardiac procedures, those of us who are lucky enough to get older do need help that we did not need before.

I think back to my father in his early forties. I look at him now, 84 years old, in what I would call terrific shape and health and mind. But even so, he's feeling it. And I remember the words of the song that was playing on the radio during that argument in a new way:

When I was younger, so much younger than today,
I never needed anybody's help in any way.
But now these days are gone, I'm not so self assured,
Now I find I've changed my mind and opened up the doors.
And now my life has changed in oh so many ways,
My independence seems to vanish in the haze.
But every now and then I feel so insecure,
I know that I just need you like I've never done before.

That's it exactly. Our lives change and we need help.

Help me, get my feet back on the ground,
Won't you please, please help me.

Think about how far down the person saying this is. They just need companionship. They appreciate people being around when they're so down. "Will you please, please help me." This admission is so difficult for so many of us. It is an admission that you cannot live independently, that you can't function on your own. Some of us are so reluctant to admit that we need help that we literally do ourselves in.

Let's talk about the children who think that their parents did for them and now they will do for their own kids but that they do not have to do anything back for their parents. This is the very structure my father taught me on the way to the barbershop. We have words for these children: selfish, self-centered, ungrateful and insensitive.

So why does this happen all the time?

I have some words for both grandparents and parents. I am newly qualified to speak about this. To the grandparents, I want to remind you of a time in your life when you had kids and ran like a chicken without a head and drove like a cabbie and it all was a blur. If you had more than one child, there can be whole parts of those years you can't even remember except that there was a maze of activity and being needed and the pressure of building up your financial lot in life.

Well, your kids are in that blur right now, so since you can remember the same period in your life, at least understand why they don't do some of the things you'd like them to do.

And to the generation of parents for whom it's all a blur right now, stop and think about your life. Maybe you don't have to give into your kid's every whim. Maybe you can have dinner at grandma's even if the kid doesn't like her meatloaf.

Both sides of the grandparent/parent divide need to stop and think a little about cutting some slack and doing better.

The relationship between parents and children has a great metaphor in the relationship between God and the Jewish people. In the Bible, there are two kinds of covenants, of sacred contracts. One is where God gives to Abraham and Abraham does not need to do much back. The covenant is basically one-way: God gives to Abraham, the way a parent gives to a small child. Later, at Mt. Sinai, a new kind of covenant is made, where God and the Israelites are in a two-way relationship: God gives and the Israelites do the Mitzvot, the Commandments, in return.

The religion of Mt. Sinai, Judaism, is supposed to be a two-way street, but for most of us, it's a one-way street: We want God to give to us and we don't do anything in return. We're God's children, and we're selfish, and we figure that He's in His prime and He's Almighty and He doesn't need anything from us anyway. So we're happy to have a one-way street and we get mad when God doesn't do exactly what we want.

But we should understand that God changed from the time of Abraham to the time when the Israelites were at Mt. Sinai. He learned that He did want a great deal in return. I can't say that His needs changed, but I can say that His demands changed.

But we don't get that. And so, like an adult child who has not adjusted to her parent's new needs and demands, we just assume that we have a one-way relationship where God gives us anything we want and we don't need to do anything in return.

We should understand that all parents, God included, want something back from their children.

This will sound cynical to you but I state it as a statement of fact: Everyone, even the most idealistic, altruistic person, wants something back.

I'll try to explain this idea by teaching you a principle from social anthropology. To have kinship is to share without reckoning. If you are my kin, I will share with you, and will give you love or things and I don't expect anything in return. That's sharing *without* reckoning. If you are not my kin, however, I will give to you and I *will* expect something in return. I share but I reckon. And if I give and I reckon and you do not give back, that is unacceptable.

So the world is divided between people who are my kin and who are not my kin. I share *without* reckoning with my kin and I share *with* reckoning with everyone else.

Anthropology is very interested in the gift, because a gift is something that I give to you, which would seem to be one-way without thinking of return. But there is supposed to be reciprocity, at least over time. You may not give me a gift in return immediately, but eventually you *should* give me something in return.

That's in anthropological theory. In reality, however, even kinship is based on sharing with reckoning. In kinship, the expectation is that eventually, what I share with you and you share with me will basically even out. I don't really think about it, because I think that I'm giving unconditionally and out of the goodness of my heart. I don't think that I'm reckoning.

But some place, deep inside of us, *is* the expectation that just as we will give to others, show up at their kid's wedding, and give the couple humongous gifts, they will give to us and be there at our big events with equally humongous gifts. And if they are not there for us like we were there for them, there will be a price to pay.

Many of our families, immediate and extended, have been destroyed through some variation of this theme. "I was there for you and cared about you but then you did not give to me or care about me." And since we only have a few great events in our lives, and they are precious to us, and we want them to be perfect, if you mar that perfection, I am *broyguss* with you, I am angry with you, forever. Maybe, if you were hit by a car and in the hospital and you still sent a great gift, *maybe* I can let it go. Otherwise, I'm done with you.

All because kinship means the expectation of reciprocity over the long haul. So when my father said, "I'm not expecting anything back from you," he meant it, inside not only that moment but where he was in his life. After all, what could this shaggy dog rebellious kid ever do for him? But underneath that tough exterior was a heart that beat very differently from his words. And that heart said, "I have done so much for this kid and no matter how he is acting now, of course I want a loving relationship for the rest of my life with him. Are you kidding? Is being a parent just raising a kid and sending him out into the world never to see him again? That's why I've spent these years sweating over every fever and every time he broke curfew and every lousy report card? Hopefully he'll turn into something better than he is now. But even if he doesn't, I'll want to be as close to him as I can possibly be."

So my father's words, and my father's heart, said two very different things.

Now let's upload this anthropological theory and this personal story to all of us in all of our relationships.

Most of the people in this world fall into the category of "I do for you and you do back for me." I pay you to render me a service. It's clean and easy and closed. I don't owe you and you don't owe me. Everything between us is counted and reckoned and finished.

But when it comes to those for whom we feel kinship, the people we care about, it's not clean and easy and closed; it's messy and complex and open-ended, *hopefully* for the rest of our lives.

Forty-one percent of baby boomers who have a living parent are providing care for them, either financial help, personal care or both. 8% say that their parents have moved in with them. Of those who are not caring for an aged parent, 37% say they expect to do so in the future. About half say they're concerned about being able to provide such care.

Thirty-four million Americans are unpaid caregivers for other adults, usually elderly relatives, and spend an average 21 hours a week helping out. Millions more grown children are calling regularly, flying into town every few weeks or months or just stopping by to take Mom or Dad to the doctor. 89% say that this is a minor sacrifice or no sacrifice at all. But they worry about being able to do what needs to be done.

This is all very hard, and such statistics hide how hard it can be and the tension these situations create. And what wrecks everything is when you don't do what I never said I expected from you and maybe even never told *myself* I expected from you. But when you don't do or say what I expected you to do and say, we've got a huge problem.

The statistics make it seem like we're not reckoning.

But a lot of us are reckoning, keeping score on numbers of phone calls and visits a week, money lent and not repaid, and so on.

We reckon all the time.

We are angry because the reckoning on our scorecards does not look the way we think it should.

We reckon all the time and we reckon in ink, without possibility of erasure.

Sharing without reckoning does not really mean unconditional one-sided sharing. God does not give to His children without wanting something back and parents do not give to their children without wanting something back, no matter what they say or think.

We think that we will never reckon, that we will continue to give to others and never need anything back from anybody. But at some point, when we're in trouble, we will need help. And if we don't get what we need, we will start reckoning as a way of life.

We're not like Bing Crosby, who didn't count sheep when he couldn't sleep but counted his blessings. We count all the bad things, over and over and over again. We don't fall asleep counting our blessings. We stay up all night counting and recounting our *grievances*. And while we're at it, we get out our scorecards that record our grievances against God and get angry at God and life itself.

So my question is: Are you a scorekeeper?

Can you share your life without reckoning?

Do you keep score about which family member or which friend did what on which date?

I'm not asking you *not* to reckon at all. You have a right to expect a general return for your sharing. But there will never be exact reciprocity in an open-ended relationship. At any given point, if you could really keep score of all the things that go on and not just remember a few things that got to you, it would really *never* be even. An open-ended good relationship between any two people *does* mean, however, that over the course of time, each does for the other according to his or her ability and receives according to his or her need.

I want to say a word to all of the tough people, the people who "don't need nobody." The truth is that, one of these days, you're going to need some help. You'll be the one who's desperate.

I've known so many people who thought that they would never need anybody's help in any way.

27

But over the years, I've seen *everyone* have their times when they needed something.

I've seen invulnerable people break in three pieces.
I've seen the strong become weak
The unflappable flapping in the wind of fear.

> *And now my life has changed in oh so many ways,*
> *My independence seems to vanish in the haze.*

And when those people needed help, sometimes their families and friends were there. And sometimes, they weren't.

And so I want to ask you a hard question: Are there people who have given to you in your life who now need help and to whom you have not given back? Don't tell me that they don't want anything back because it's *not true*. From each according to his or her ability and to each according to his or her need.

It's very simple: Help when you should and receive help when you need it. And stop keeping score. Stop *reckoning* so much.

Once, my father went through an operation for a tumor on his lung. After the operation, the surgeon came out and said that the prognosis was grim at best. A few horrible days later, the results showed that the tumor was benign and that my father was perfectly healthy. But the experience had knocked my father for a physical and emotional loop, and he came up here to Connecticut for a while. When he felt ready to go home, I took him to the airport, and he said to me, "I took care of you. Now you took care of me."

He seemed so different from the guy who took me to the barbershop. But of course, he was the same guy. There are different moments and different times in our lives.

Thank God that was twenty-five years ago, and he's been great since then.

Should I have said to my father at the airport, "You're welcome, but just for the record:
"I remember how you drove me against my will to get that haircut;
How you laughed as I was shorn of my virility;
How you *glowed* as I was shorn of my *hippiness* and my happiness;
How you violated my personal rights;
I blame you to this day for the fact that I lost my chance forever with Linda Sternfeld."

Should I have checked the scoreboard and read a hundred such grievances to reckon if I should be of help when he was down?

Of course not.

Should I have said, "But you taught me that I was supposed to take care of my kids and I didn't have to worry about you?"

Of course not.

Instead I muttered something like, "I'm happy I could help."

My prayer for all of us is that we work very, very hard, with everything we have, to have relationships in which we give and receive, lives in which we couldn't reckon if we wanted to, because our love for each other has made our lives so full of giving and receiving that we don't know where the circle begins.

Chapter Four

You Are Entitled to Your Opinion, but You're Not Entitled to Your Own Facts

We are in a high school class in U.S. History, somewhere in Connecticut, 2007. A student says, "The slave trade of Africans to America never really happened." Other students look at him with curiosity. "Yes," he says, "this whole subject has been grossly exaggerated by American blacks to explain their difficult experience in this country and to win compassion. Africans really wanted to come to America, eagerly and voluntarily got on ships, and came over here, hiring themselves out on plantations for fair wages and good treatment and better lives."

What would you expect the teacher to say in response? Let's say that when other students replied that the student doesn't know what he's talking about, the teacher said, "Now, now, boys and girls, he's entitled to his opinion."

What if a teacher at a public high school allowed that remark denying the trade in African slaves to America to stand without refutation, to be called one opinion among others, validating the possibility of its truth?

How long would it take for that teacher to be fired? If that teacher did not absolutely and categorically refute and disprove the student's remark denying the slave trade, he or she would be hounded as a racist. And indeed, that teacher would **not** be worthy of being called a history teacher. History is about understanding the past. To deny the facts of the past is to undermine the study of history.

But what if the same student, and it would be the same kind of prejudiced and moronic student, said that the Holocaust never happened. And the teacher said, "Well, there are many people across the world who agree with that and many others who think that the number six million is grossly exaggerated." What would happen to that teacher?

Apparently nothing, because, guess what? It happens all across the country. Students can say, "I don't believe the Holocaust really happened" or "My father says that the Holocaust is just a big myth" or "I read on the Internet that the Holocaust is a lie." And teachers say, "He's entitled to his opinion." The teacher will respect that opinion, and if another student argues, it is left open as a debate.

The late great Senator Daniel Patrick Moynihan said, "You are entitled to your opinion, but you're not entitled to your own facts." That's what every teacher should say.

It's stupefying: We are talking about the best-documented event in human history. There is a facility housed in a town in central Germany known as the International Tracing Service, which houses **30 million pieces of paper on 16 miles of shelves**. It is the largest repository of Holocaust documents in the world. It's all there, from the colored index cards the Gestapo kept on millions of citizens to the identity cards issues to forced laborers, including the deportation record of Anne Frank and the lists of slave laborers rescued by Oskar Schindler. There are cabinets of precise, handwritten records of executions that fill pages of lined composition notebooks from death camps. 48 people were shot at two-minute intervals on April 20, 1942 as a present to Hitler on his birthday. The SS wrote it all down, every detail.

At Yad Vashem in Jerusalem, the most important museum to the Holocaust, I saw film footage of the poor starving children in the Warsaw Ghetto; children falling in the street from hunger and sickness, children in tattered rags. And I asked the question: "How do we have this record?" The answer was that the Nazis themselves filmed the children, and showed these films in the movie theaters in Germany. When people tell you that the Germans didn't know what was going on, don't you believe it for one second. The Nazis were proud to show the starving, dying Jewish children in the movie theatres. They kept careful records of every kind. The Nazis didn't deny the Holocaust; they proclaimed it and advertised it and were triumphant and gleeful about every Jewish person killed.

So to say that the Holocaust didn't happen or is any way exaggerated is pure and utter nonsense of a very evil kind. And yet, from a local high school to a conference of evil in Iran to newspapers around the globe to the Internet where people write anything they want and get away with it, people say it all the time.

Now you say: "Why make a big deal? Everyone with a brain knows that the Holocaust happened." I would respond that people with brains are being indoctrinated right this minute all around the world. People with brains know what they are taught and what they read. And if they are taught and if they read that the Holocaust never happened or was grossly exaggerated, then that's exactly what they think.

Or you might say, that's all very sad, but if we're talking about history, about events that happened over sixty years ago, what difference does this make for the world today?

Let me explain how the denial of the Holocaust is part and parcel of what is going on in the world today and how the denial of the Holocaust changes how we, and I mean you and I, see the world today.

People tell me that Israel is wrong not to work out a peace deal with the Palestinians. Many very nice people think, to quote the expert on current affairs, A. J. Soprano, that no one even knows how the Israeli-Palestinian conflict started, that it's about a cycle of violence that goes around and around and it's about borders and it's about territories and it's about occupation.
Their first mistake is in thinking that Israel would not sign a decent peace treaty today if there was a chance of having peace and security. People distinguish between the terrorist party Hamas, the party that controls the Palestinian government in Gaza, and the supposedly moderate President Mahmoud Abbas, who controls the West Bank.

So let's do a little exercise. Let's ask the question: What does Hamas say about the Holocaust, and then, what does the moderate President Abbas say about the Holocaust? If you understand what people say about the Holocaust, you get the true picture of who they are.

Hamas has in its charter that the Holocaust is a fake. In Article 22 of the Hamas Charter the Jews are blamed for the French Revolution, World War I, the Communist revolution, World War II and those sinister organizations – the Masons, the Rotary Club and the Lions. Hamas says that the Holocaust is a myth perpetrated by Jewish people for their own financial gains. It says that Jewish people distort the facts. But of course it is the Holocaust deniers who distort the facts and then say that Jewish people distort the facts.

And this is just the beginning of their hatred.

The director of the Hamas Children's Summer Camp in Gaza City stated: "The first thing we want to teach the children is their cause. They know from daily experience that their enemy is the Jew — our job is to explain why. In the Koran much is said about the bad behavior of the Jew ... God cursed the Jews."

In April 2007, Dr. Ahmad Bahar, acting Hamas speaker of the Palestinian Legislative Council, referred to Israel's Jewish citizens as a "cancerous lump" and prays to Allah to "count them and kill them to the last one, and don't leave even one."

So that's what Hamas thinks. It could not be clearer. What about the so-called moderate Abbas? He wrote his doctoral dissertation, his Ph.D. thesis, on this

32

topic and later published it as a book with the title: *The Other Face: The Secret Connection between the Nazis and the Zionist Movement*. Abbas says that the entire Zionist movement collaborated with the Nazis in the annihilation of the Jewish people.[1] Abbas also denies that the gas chambers were for murdering people, and claims that they were only for incinerating bodies, out of concern for the spread of disease and infection in the region.

So we did our exercise. The Palestinians, both Hamas and Abbas, both the explicit killers and the so-called moderate faction, deny the Holocaust.

Do you think that such people really want to negotiate and make peace?

How can you negotiate with people who lie about facts?

How can you trust in what such people say about the future when you know that they lie about the past?

In the face of all of the evidence, why should anyone deny the Holocaust?

To say that Jewish people do not get to be victims worthy of compassion. Why? So that they themselves can claim to be the victims of the Jews.

Their problem with Israel has nothing to do with borders or treaties or territories, it has nothing to do with the facts, only the evil opinion that Jewish

[1] Abu Mazen discusses the question of the number of Jewish Holocaust victims, denying commonly accepted data. He writes:

> After WWII, it was announced that 6 million Jews were among the victims, and that the war of annihilation had been aimed first of all against the Jews, and only then against the rest of the peoples of Europe. It seems that the Zionist movement's stake in inflating the number of murdered in the war aimed at [ensuring] great gains. This led it to confirm the number [6 million], to establish it in world opinion, and by doing so to arouse more pangs of conscience and sympathy for Zionism in general. Many scholars have debated the question of the 6 million figure, and reached perplexing conclusions, according to which the Jewish victims total hundreds of thousands.... To date, no proof whatsoever exists that the number of Jewish victims in the Nazi concentration camps reached four million or six million. In effect, the true number is much smaller than these fictitious millions." The [American] historian and author Raul Hilberg thinks that this number is no greater than 896,000."

Just for the record, Abu Mazen's attribution of this figure to Raul Hillberg's *The Destruction of the European Jews* is false.

33

people shouldn't live and certainly shouldn't have their own country. Because if Jewish people have their own country they will have an army and if they have an army they will protect themselves and they will not be killed.

Why do they deny the undeniable?
They deny *the Holocaust* to hide the fact that it is exactly what they want to do.

They want to be the greatest Jew-killers in history and they can't stand the competition.

Anti-Semites always accuse us of doing what they are doing.[2] We're not the ones fighting all over the globe. It is Muslims who are anti-West, anti-Democracy, anti-Christian, anti-Jewish, anti-Buddhist, and anti-Hindu. I may be off by a war or two, but Muslims are involved in 25 of the 30 conflicts going on in the world today.[3]

So they say, as found in the Hamas Charter: "There is no war going on anywhere without Jewish people having their finger in it."

They say it's us, but the facts show that it's them. They blame us of doing what they're doing.

You say, "Why bother me about these kinds of people? They are just evil." But I want to correct you: They are not the only deniers of the Holocaust.

We are also, in our own way, Holocaust deniers.

For example, we hear that people are being killed in the Sudan, and we don't do anything and we don't say anything. We deny the fact of genocide.

Some of the people who will read this are Holocaust-deniers and do not support Israel. They spout ignorant platitudes. For example, a nice Jewish girl in my community, a recent college graduate, said, "The Jewish people never had any trouble before Israel existed."

This has to be the most ignorant statement anyone ever made. Why do you think there is an Israel? Because the Jewish people in Europe and the Arab

---

[2] For example, the man who accused Captain Alfred Dreyfus (France, 1896) of spying was the one who was the spy.
[3] In Afghanistan, Algeria, Bangladesh, Bosnia, Congo, Cote d'Ivoire, Cyprus, East Timor, India, Indonesia (2 provinces), Kashmir, Kazakhstan, Kosovo, Kurdistan, Macedonia, the Middle East, Nigeria, Pakistan, Philippines, Sudan, Russia-Chechnya, Tajikistan, Thailand, Uganda and Uzbekistan.

countries were so happy and were treated so well? Did she ever hear of the Holocaust? Doesn't she understand that the attacks on Israel are part of Hitler's program?

If you are like this girl, do yourself and everybody else a favor.

Don't just buy the propaganda. Read. Learn.

When people think that Israel has problems because it controls Arab territories, they should learn that before Israel won those territories in 1967, the PLO carried out terrorist attacks in 1964, 1965, and 1966 when Israel was in possession of *no territories whatsoever*. We forget that a victorious Israel immediately offered to return Sinai to Egypt and the Golan to Syria only to be met with the Arab League's famous three "nos": no peace, no recognition and no negotiation.

We forget that if the Palestinians had wanted a viable state of their own, they could have had it a long time ago.

Anti-Semites say: "Jews control all the money in the world."
I wish it were true. If we did, there wouldn't be poverty or hunger or homelessness.

Anti-Semites say: "Jews control the media." OK, I get it. We control the media, which is why the world is influenced by media that is so anti-Israel and anti-Semitic. I wish we did control the media to counter the propaganda that is so Anti-Israel that Americans from a sanctimonious collaborator with evil named Jimmy Carter to millions and millions of ignorant and misinformed people believe a pack of lies.

It is difficult for me when anyone spouts Anti-Semitism.
But when it's Jewish people who do it, trying to sound oh-so-hip and oh-so-cool, I have only one description for them:
They are Holocaust-deniers.

I am not just embarrassed; I am ashamed.

I am ashamed in front of the memories of a million and a half children who were killed not just by the Nazis but also by people of many other countries.

A million and a half children.
What had any of them done?
Were they soldiers?
Were they terrorists?

And that girl says that the Jewish people never had any problems until there was a State of Israel?

I am ashamed of the Jewish knee-jerk liberals who say that they just want to give peace a chance and who don't understand that Israel has never wanted anything but peace and has always given peace every possible chance.

They are entitled to their own opinions but they are not entitled to their own facts.

When I left Yad Vashem with a recent tour, I asked each of the people in the group to give me one word on their mind. One of the young people said, "Education." I couldn't agree more. Maybe we could get rid of some of the misguided opinions if people were guided to the facts. But my worry about education, and this is a general concern for me, is that kids learn isolated facts so that they can take a test, that the Holocaust becomes another set of facts, another course, and that very few integrate that knowledge into wisdom about the present. Knowledge must be transformed into the wisdom to understand this world.

And another young man said at Yad Vashem: "I feel isolated not by my Jewishness but by the failure of others to comprehend what has gone on and is going on now."

That's exactly how I feel. I feel isolated because the world seems to be split into three parts, with the Holocaust as a kind of moral litmus test:

One part says that the Holocaust never happened or was exaggerated. These people are evil.

A second part says that the Holocaust happened but either doesn't care, or is bored by the subject. These people are not evil but they do not see evil.

And a third part of the world, which includes many Jewish people, says that the Holocaust happened and was horrible beyond belief and that we must be sure it never happens again, but does not apply this understanding to the current situations in the world.

And that leaves some of us, a very few of us, screaming in frustration that nobody gets it, that another Holocaust is ready to happen at any of a number of places in this world right this minute. We're like Harry Potter who, when no one believed him that evil was very real, had to marshal all his inner resources to insist that evil was true and dangerous.

And again I say to the nice people who will read this that your niceness blinds you into denial, that many of us do not deny the Holocaust but deny its meaning, deny its implications.

But if we deny the meaning of the Holocaust, if we think it was a one-time event, we will break our bond with the people who died at the hands of evil and we *risk* the lives of the people of this world at the hands of those who are quite eager to destroy us.

Evil counts on the weakness of the good, preying on our goodness, negotiating with treachery, depending on our hopes for peace, making agreements that they will never live by.

It's hard to think about evil and not despair.

But ask the Holocaust survivors and their children who are alive today.

Evil is real and must be countered with strength and resolve.

TO DENY THE HOLOCAUST IS NOT JUST TO DENY A HISTORICAL EVENT.

TO DENY THE HOLOCAUST IS NOT JUST TO DENY THE RIGHT OF ISRAEL TO EXIST.

TO DENY THE HOLOCAUST IS TO DENY THE RIGHT OF JEWISH PEOPLE TO LIVE AT ALL.

Tell the truth about those who deny the Holocaust.

The same people who deny the Holocaust are the people who want another Holocaust.

And then there are people who deny evil and allow evil to flourish.

Don't you be one of them.

Stand up for truth when you hear lies.

When you hear people denying the Holocaust or rejecting Israel or failing to apply what we've learned about evil to our situation in the world today, tell them:

You are entitled to your opinion, but you are not entitled to your own facts.

Chapter Five

Because of You: An American Idol in the Pit

You may have heard of a television show called *American Idol,* certainly one of the most popular cultural phenomena in America in recent years. When it comes to elections, Americans often make mistakes by voting their likes and dislikes over any other consideration. But in the first year of the competition, a young woman named Kelly Clarkson was the popular choice, and in this case, the country got it right. In fact, Kelly Clarkson has turned out to be more talented than anyone ever imagined. She is a great singer and a fine songwriter. Her best song is called "Because of You." It is an unusual song; it's not about romantic love but about a daughter's relationship with her mother. If you listen, you find it wrenching and devastating. You are moved with compassion not just for the young woman who writes and sings this song but for every child who has experienced similar emotional trauma.

Kelly Clarkson says that because of her mother, she has taught herself not to love or trust, so that she will not experience the pain of being hurt. Her heart cannot break, she says, because it was not whole to start with. When she was a child, she had to listen to her mother cry every night. Her mother let her see everything; she leaned on her young daughter inappropriately. Her mother was so consumed with her own pain that she couldn't think about anyone else. And so now as an adult the daughter sings:

Because of you I never strayed too far from the sidewalk
Because of you I learned to play on the safe side so I don't get hurt
Because of you I try my hardest just to forget everything
Because of you I don't know how to let anyone else in

She's so scared of life that she stays on the sidewalk, like a little child. She's so scared of life that she will not let herself fall in love.

The problem with this song is that it never progresses. There is conflict but no resolution. Art is about expression, but *great* art also teaches a moral lesson. This song is a powerful expression but it never helps us to rise. We go down into the pit with the singer and we never come out.

How different this is from the essential Jewish songs. In the Biblical Book of Psalms, there are many songs of distress and complaint. According to superscriptions placed before some of these psalms, they were written by or for King David. We see David in a cave, David trapped, David fleeing for his life;

the common thread is that we see David in trouble and in despair. But this is David and we know his life. We know that he will go on and become the greatest king in our history. We know that when he describes his situation and when he trusts in God and when he does not give up and when he has hope and acts on that hope, he will *emerge*, he will prevail, he will succeed. These psalms are songs that we can relate to because they express what it means to be desperate. People who are spiritual read the Psalms a lot, especially those psalms that start at the bottom and climb in hope. That's why the Psalms are more significant than popular songs; they express our pain but they also teach us how to live. The Psalms say that the way out of bad situations is to have faith in God and in the power of hope.

These psalms remind me of the story of the man who falls and finds himself in a dark pit. And he cries out in the darkness. And then, at the top of the pit, there's another man.
"Throw me down a rope!" he calls up hopefully. Instead, the other man climbs down into the darkness with him.
"Why didn't you throw me a rope?" he asks. "Now what are we going to do?"
"I didn't have a rope," the man says, "but I've been down here before and I know the way out."

Kelly Clarkson doesn't seem to know the way out.

She's down in the pit and she's staying down there and that's the whole story.

Judaism, represented by the psalms of David, knows the way out.

The American Idol has lost her ability to trust. I don't blame her. I feel very badly for her. She's had it very rough. But the truth is that you have to go on. Not just go on, but learn whom you can trust, and learn what and who to believe in.

If anyone has experience of being in the pit because they've been down there before, it's the Jewish people.
We were slaves in Egypt for hundreds of years.
We have been locked in ghettos.
We have been exiled from our homes over and over again.
We have been discriminated against, persecuted, systematically murdered.
Shouldn't we be like Kelly Clarkson? Shouldn't we say to the world:

> *Because of you we don't know how to let anyone else in*
> *Because of you we're afraid to trust in anyone*
> *Because of you we're frightened to be ourselves*

We have every right to ask: "After all of these centuries of being hurt and killed, can we trust anyone else?" The Jews of Germany had climbed into the highest reaches of society. Reform Judaism was created in 19th century Germany where Jewish people said, "We're not going to wear *yalmulkas*, we're not going to think about Israel, we're going to play an organ in our services, because we want to be like everyone else, we want to be good Germans." They were patriotic Germans, and we all know what happened.

So you can't blame us if, like Kelly Clarkson, we have trust issues.

The best introduction to these issues for modern Jewish people is a popular novel that remains a very important book, Leon Uris' *Exodus*. The underlying question is: After the Holocaust, can the builders of modern Israel trust anyone? Can they trust the Arabs? Can they trust the other countries of the world? *Exodus* gives us three answers, represented by three of the main characters.

Akiva ben Canaan, a fictionalized version of Menachem Begin, the head of the radical organization Irgun and later Prime Minister of Israel, says: "Look at the Holocaust. The world did nothing. We cannot trust anyone." He's in the pit and he has not come out.

Akiva's brother Barak ben Canaan, who represents the leaders of the Labor Party like David ben Gurion, says, "We must trust others and try to work things out, no matter what has happened." He is a messenger of hope.

Ari ben Canaan, the one played by Paul Newman in the movie, is the nephew of Akiva and the son of Barak, and he knows that both of them are right: The Jewish people *cannot trust*; the Jewish people *must* trust.

If you want to understand Israel, even these decades later, I beg you to read or re-read the novel *Exodus*. Even the movie, for all of its limitations, gets right to the heart of the problem: Can you trust? Can Jewish people trust other people?

To which I respond with a simple formula:
Prepare for the worst but hope for the best.
Prepare for the worst but hope for the best.
Don't risk your life, but be willing to risk your pride.
Build a fence to protect yourself, but keep reaching out to others.

By the way, you'll notice that when Israel built a fence to protect its children against homicide bombers, the world cried foul.

But when America built a fence to keep out peaceful illegal immigrants, the world said nothing.

Why is this? Because every country has the right and the duty to protect itself, except Israel. Israel has no right to protect itself. Why is this? Because Jewish life is expendable. Akiva ben Canaan *was* right: The world does *not* care. But he wasn't right to give up, because that means always staying in the pit of loneliness, of distrust.

That was Israel, 1948. So what does Israel do in 2006? Israel is still Ari ben Canaan, the Lion of the land of Canaan, after these decades of war and terrorism, struggling within itself, within its very soul, between trusting and not trusting.

Don't put your life in the hands of your enemies. They'll kill you without a second thought. Continue to work for peace, but from a position of strength.

And so we have every right to be scared.

And yet, we continue to believe; we continue to look forward.
Hope is necessary.

Let me turn from the example of Israel back to examples from our lives.

Think about this passage from an incredible novel called *The Attack* by Yasmina Khadra.

> *When you're young and starting out and you haven't learned the hard lessons of life and trust, you think you've got the world by the tail. You think you know everything. You think that everything is just terrific and that all people are wonderful. You're confident. Life is smiling on you. So is luck. You love and are loved. You can afford your dreams. Everything's fine, everyone blesses you. And then, without warning, the sky falls in on your head. And once you're flat on your back, you realize that your life, your whole life - with its ups and downs, its pains and pleasures, its promises and failures - hangs and has always hung by a thread as flimsy and imperceptible as the threads in a spider's web. Suddenly, the slightest sound terrifies you and you no longer feel like believing in anything whatsoever. All you want to do is close your eyes and think no more.* [Yasmina Khadra, *The Attack*, translated by John Cullen (2006).]

Do you understand these feelings? Have there been times you've felt this way? But you kept going, didn't you? How did you do it? How did you keep going?

41

Let me tell you how one person did it. A young woman comes to see me. Her husband, whom she loves very much, has one foot out the door. He says he doesn't love her anymore. She's in the darkness of the pit. We talk for a while, and she talks about her dreams that are in pieces on the floor. But then she looks up and says: "If this happens, I'm going to get married again. I believe in my power to love. I want to be loved." Like Kelly Clarkson, she's suffered a trauma of trust. But unlike the singer, she's not going to give up on love. Her words are like the psalms: She's in the pit but she knows the way out. She cannot trust the man who has been her husband, because for whatever reason, legitimate or not, fair or not, he's leaving. She doesn't trust him, but she wants to trust someone else. She doesn't trust right now, but she keeps her hope alive.

That's trusting in God. That even if you don't get what you deserve. The values are right. God's ways are right.

There are things about which we simply have to trust in God. But there are other things with which God has entrusted us, to live our lives in the right way.

So what's the way to climb out of the pit? By trusting in *God* and trusting in *yourself.*

To trust in God means to hope.

Sometimes I think that Hope, the Hebrew word *tikvah,* is the very name of God, the meaning of God. We hope, we pray that things will get better. We pray that the human condition itself, this whole sequence of getting old and sick and dying, will change radically.

That's what the belief in the Messiah is about. When the Messiah comes, there will be no more wars or death.

There may be a billion people who believe that the Messiah came a couple of thousand years ago. But we know that there is still sickness and there are wars and there is death, so that doesn't make any sense to us; the Messiah, *unfortunately,* has *not* come yet. But we're hoping, not so much in the coming of a person as in the advent of an age when there will be peace and health for all.

Ani maamin be-emunah shlemah
ve af al pi sheyeetmahmayah
eem kol zeh ani maamin

I believe with a perfect faith that the Messiah will come
And even though he tarries, even so, I believe.

Until the Messiah comes, we will live in a world that is filled with evil, horrible evil, like terrorism and murder and genocide.

But we also live in a world filled with the lesser evils:
The daily evils of people who will trick you; fool you, steal from you.
The daily evils of those who will step on you to climb another rung of the ladder.
The lesser evils of people who envy you;
The lesser evils of those who will gossip about you without basis simply because they have lurid imaginations.

Don't tell me you don't know what I'm talking about.
You get to a point where you wonder if you can trust anyone at all.

And if you have suffered a trauma of trust, if you have discovered that you should never have trusted someone on whom you based your life, then what? How do you trust again?

Prepare for the worst and hope for the best.

Okay, so what is the *best* thing that can happen?

The best thing would be if despite all of your doubts about human nature, you *could* find a person whom you *can* trust.
Isn't it amazing when you find even one person in this world in whom you *can* have complete and utter confidence?

Isn't it reassuring when you find someone that you can trust with your life?

Doesn't it give you a wonderful sense of security when you know that you can rely on someone to take care of the lives of your children if some disaster would befall you?

And isn't it something when you so completely trust a person that you would be willing to sign over everything you had in the world, your money, your home, your possessions, knowing that it would be in good and safe hands and would be returned whenever you said?

That even if they give you the wrong advice, they were giving you the best advice they have?

But trusting someone with your life, your money, your children is not what I'm really thinking about.

It's trusting people with your *heart* that's my real issue. What a feeling to be able to trust someone with your emotions! You can take all of your fears, your concerns, your joys; you can take all of your eggs, put them in someone else's basket, and they won't be dropped.

No matter how you feel, you know that the person will be with you, in good times and bad, no matter what you do or how you do it.

If you have one or more people like that in your life, don't take them for granted and realize that you're blessed.

I go back to the woman who sat there crushed because her husband was leaving her. She still believed in love. And she also believed in herself, she trusted herself.

What a wonderful thing.

Maybe trusting yourself is even harder than trusting another person.

Believing in yourself means that you can do it, that, even if it's all by yourself, you will find the way out of the pit.

And if you're in the pit, there is this voice,
symbolized by an Israel that continues to work for peace against all odds,
symbolized by the man who came down into the pit because he knew the way out,
symbolized by King David in the Psalms who started in the pit and trusted in God and climbed out,
if you're in the pit there is this voice,
and it is the voice of God.

And if you're not in the pit,

and I pray to God that you're not,

and you have people in your life whom you can trust, tell them sometimes:

Because of you I always know that someone is on my side.
Because of you I'm not alone.
I have a life worth living because of you.

Chapter Six

The Shunning or The No-Suspenders vs. Two-Suspenders Debate

I want to tell you a story about two brothers. They lived in Lancaster, Pennsylvania among the most conservative branch of the Amish, a sect of the so-called Pennsylvania Dutch.[1] The two brothers, Uriah and Amos Stolzfus, were known as the "Stoltzfus boys." They had inherited a wonderful, large and productive farm that their family had owned for four centuries. They had a wonderful life and a great livelihood.

Again, they belonged to the most fundamentalist branch of the Amish, which taught, among other things, that if a man wore suspenders to secure his trousers he was guilty of vanity and an addiction to self-adornment. The men in the group held their pants up with ropes, used pins instead of buttons, and wore heavy beards. Some of the more liberal members of the congregation proposed a compromise: "Since suspenders are more effective than rope in holding up a man's pants, we authorize them, but the man must wear only one brace over whichever shoulder he likes, because to wear two would be an act of vanity."

The younger brother Amos was a freethinker. He didn't like the anti-suspender rule and he didn't go for the compromise, either. He insisted on suspenders with two braces. Even worse, he was also caught buying store-made clothes instead of having his wife sew everything by hand.

This was absolutely forbidden, and it was his older brother Uriah who led the charge against him. The brothers fought terribly, with the conservative brother Uriah goading his more liberal brother Amos so terribly that the fight became known in the area as "no-suspenders brother against two-suspenders brother." Shock waves swept not only their congregation but the whole Amish community. This went on for years.

Eventually, Uriah was so outraged that his younger brother would challenge his principles that he personally led a movement to ostracize Amos. It was called "shunning." It was a terrible punishment, for it banned the person from even talking to other members of the congregation. Amos could not talk to

---

[1] By the way, the Pennsylvania Dutch are not Dutch but Germans; they were the Pennsylvania Deutsch, Germans, which in American vernacular became Pennsylvania Dutch.

anyone, meet with them, eat with them, buy or sell from them, or worship with them. The ostracism was total, and what was even worse was that Amos was now married and had children. Amos' wife and children were told that they could not have anything to do with him or the congregation would shun them, too. Amos and his wife weren't going to deal with this, so they left the farm that was half theirs and moved to Reading, Pennsylvania. Amos shaved, affiliated with a Mennonite church, and opened a livery stable. He prospered financially. He had modern conveniences such as an icebox.

But as the years passed, Amos thought less about the money they were making and more about their happy days as members of an Amish community. Every autumn when the harvest was in, Amos sent a humble letter to his church begging it to cancel his shunning so that he might resume the membership he and his wife longed for. When the first letter arrived, in 1901, the elderly head of the congregation said: "According to Amish rules, a member shunned can be rejoined to the church, but only if he comes back, throws himself on his hands and knees before the church leader, admits his sin and pleads for reinstatement." When Amos received this verdict, he told his wife, "Fair enough. I was headstrong years ago, and if this is the rule for repentance, I accept." But in the meantime, who had become leader of the congregation to whom Amos must bow and scrape and show tears in his eyes? None other than his brother Uriah, whose tyranny had led to the banishment in the first place. Since Amos refused to humble himself before his self-righteous brother, he stayed excommunicated, shunned by all good Amish who wore no suspenders.

More years passed and Amos and his son converted the livery stable into a garage. Amos became a very prosperous businessman and was very well regarded in Mennonite society. But his enormous loss ate into his soul. Spiritually, he was an Amish man who wanted to die in the embrace of his church, but each year, as his wealth increased, he fell further away from his austere faith. Each new modern device he purchased made it more unlikely that he would turn back, but even so, he continued to send annual begging letters to his old church and each year the official letter reminded him of the rules. The letter never reminded Amos that the head of the church who would judge him and before whom he must crawl was still his brother Uriah, but Amos knew this, and he would not submit.

Amos would slip back into Lancaster sometimes, to secretly view the farm that his family had owned through four different centuries and which he had worked so hard to improve. Amos would sit there at night, in the darkness, alone with his thoughts, and he would blame *himself* for his stubbornness about the suspenders that had prevented him from ever assuming responsibility for that beautiful land again. In the end, Amos died in exile.

The story I just told you is from a novel called *The Novel* by the famous author James Michener. This story resonates with me in several different ways. It is a story about religion, but it is also a story about two members of a family. Uriah was wrong in so many ways: as a person, as a leader, and especially as a brother. The poignant part for me is how Amos, despite the cruel treatment that he had received from his brother and his community, would have been willing to ask forgiveness for simply living the way the rest of the world did. He was willing to swallow all of his pride, except that which had to do with his brother. What the congregation did to him was not personal; they did what they believed. But Amos was not willing to bow down to his brother Uriah, who had mercilessly led the community against him.

Review those personal relationships that have gone badly in your life and make sure that *you* are not playing the part of Uriah. When it comes to our family feuds, and let's face it, almost all of us have family members from whom we're estranged, we are very agile in our reasoning. We're always sure that it's all his or her fault. *We* are never to blame. We are the innocent Amos, and they are Uriah. But guess what? That member of your family whom you're not talking to thinks that he or she is Amos and that *you* are Uriah. Once in a while, for everyone's sake, ask yourself a tough question: Could the problem be me?

Once in a while, when I'm really being an adult, I recognize that I'm at fault. It doesn't feel very good. I don't like to blame myself. It doesn't feel very good at all. But once I come to that realization, I understand that just as I've contributed to creating a bad situation, I may have a chance to fix it. Sometimes, once I take responsibility, it's amazing how everything else can fall into place. It's easy to play Amos, the one who has been insulted, the innocent victim. But I have to recognize that sometimes, as weird as this is for me, I'm Uriah. When I am, it's up to me to do something.

The story of Uriah and Amos works on that personal level but it also resonates in terms of our relationships to Judaism. You see, we can make fun of a fight about suspenders all we want, but there was something important involved in that debate; the issue of a religion's relationship to the past. The fight was not about suspenders but about whether to be a part of a world that is consumed with vanity and change. "No suspenders vs. two-suspenders" sounds absolutely ridiculous, and it *is* absolutely ridiculous, but symbolically speaking, both sides had something very important to say.

Uriah was saying, "We will not become a part of an ever-changing world. We don't need suspenders. We don't need to get caught up in the personal vanity of modern clothes."

And Amos was saying, "Maybe *you* won't but *I* will. Suspenders represent my wish to be a part of the world. Suspenders don't imply that I don't revere God or respect the past. I do. But suspenders are an improvement on rope."

Uriah and the community that shunned Amos were wrong to be stuck in the past. I am a person who believes in the approach of Conservative Judaism. In Conservative Judaism, we really don't care if you wear suspenders or belts, though if you just wear a rope you'll probably push me to the end of mine. We believe that you can dress like everyone around you, as long as those people are dressing appropriately in terms of modesty and the occasion at hand. Like Amos, we feel that it is proper to make changes, to live in the current century. We have not been preoccupied with the past as an issue in itself. Ask me to list the changes that the Conservative movement has made in its entire history and I can count them on my fingers. Most of the changes are not changes in the rituals at all but simply allowing females to participate in those rituals.

Orthodox people would say that the debate between Orthodox and Conservative Judaism over women's rights is not about respect for women but about respect for the past. They say that it's a game of dominoes, that if you change the laws about women's rights, all of Judaism will come crashing down. The objectively fascinating thing is that Orthodoxy has seen a resurgence in our time, building real communities of people who observe the commandments. Females who believe that they are equal to males in every way are willing to sit on the other side of a curtain and to be treated as second-class citizens because they have bought the line that it is all or nothing; that either we accept everything from the past or we will not have a vibrant Jewish community.

Amos joined a Mennonite church and found a community that was traditional but allowed him to dress as he pleased. He had a good life. He was prosperous. So why did he want to come back to a community that had shunned him? Amos, the great two-suspenders rebel himself, struggled with his relationship to the past. He came to realize that his past, represented by his farm and his community, had great meaning and beauty. He wanted to come home.

The richness of the story, the poignant part of this story, is when Amos sneaks home in the darkness of night to stare at the fields of his past, of his youth. That's the part that haunts me.

I wonder if you understand that part of the story. You may think that he missed his home, but he misses more than that.

I'm sure you like hearing that Amos rebelled against the rigidity of his community's technical rules. But how do you feel about the fact that he was willing to get down on his knees and beg forgiveness for that very rebellion? Amos is a hero to us because he was willing to rebel, but his life has a tragic dimension. He made a choice, and we applaud him, but there is something deeply unsatisfying about his life, and he knows it so well that if not for his intolerant brother, he'd give up his suspenders and the icebox and the garage and get down on his knees to get his past back.

Why is it this way? Why is it a choice between living in the past and giving up the beauty and meaning of our religion? The whole point of Conservative Judaism is that Amos faced a false choice. We do not have to choose between living entirely in the past and giving up our religion. Conservative Judaism does not believe for a second that we should be stuck in the past.

Conservative Judaism says that we can live in modern times, we can learn from the best of what today offers us, and we can remain true to our rituals and our principles and our beliefs.

Here's the sad part: Conservative Judaism generally has failed to create a community of people who have true respect for the past and for our rituals. But what's even *worse* is that most of us Conservative Jews don't even get the *problem*. We simply do what we want to do when we want to do it. And there's little to no respect for the past in all its richness. Most of us sitting here today have never even *seen* that beautiful farm.

Amos left one community and found another one. His story, as sad as it is, is not *as* sad as the story of most of *our* lives. We have not gone from one community to another. We have gone from one community to no community.

A quick example: I'm sitting at a wedding reception recently, and a man comes over to me and says, "I don't get why some of these people were invited." I ask him what he means. He says that he doesn't know what the connection is between the family involved and some of the guests. When he mentions certain individuals, I explain that all of them are people who either come to services or are involved in our shul in some way. And he hears that, and he thinks about it for a minute, and then he says, "Wow. I'll have to think about that." And I say, "That's what it can be." He had never realized that the synagogue could provide one with the friends who matter so much to you that they're the ones you want near you at the key moments of your life. He had never realized that by seeing each other all the time at shul, relationships and kinship had developed, a feeling of family had grown. It struck him; it was a "wow," a new thought, that deep relationships can be created through community bonding.

I want to say something else about the community formed by a synagogue. During the years when my boys were in the Hamden Little League, I would be one of those parents who would try to go to every game and support my kids. And the other parents who shared that value were very friendly. We went through victories and defeats together, and we liked each other. That was a nice thing, a feeling of community spirit.

But then our boys grew up, and except for maybe a chance encounter at the grocery store, I never see any of those people. That was what I call a *temporary* community.

The synagogue, on the opposite pole, is a *permanent* community. It is a community for all stages of your life, every season of your life. What it can provide for you will change as you change, and that's a good thing.

That's why Amos wanted the community of his older years to be the same one that he had in his youth.

Amos struggled with his choice. Conservative Judaism, in trying to create real communities, wrestles with the choices we have to make to find a balance between the past and the present. We have enough respect and humility before the wisdom of the past that if we're going to consider a change, we go very, very slowly and lie awake wondering if it's the right decision.

Struggle is the key word. If you're going to be a true Conservative Jewish person you must first understand how difficult the struggle is. If you are willing to forget thousands of years of wisdom and heritage and meaning, if you can just throw that all away without a care, you don't get it.

So let me break it down for you. I'll present you with the clear choices that Modern Judaism offers you. I'll briefly define the three main movements of Modern Judaism and their very different positions about the past.

Orthodoxy claims to present a Judaism that is 100% true to the past. That, in a sense, is the position of Uriah, and the no-suspenders rule represents how duplicating the details of the past often overwhelm everything else.

Reform claims to be the Judaism of Abraham, an ethical monotheist, a moral man who believed in one God. Reform Judaism says that we can start at 0% of the past and choose whatever we want as long as we are good people.

Conservative Judaism is an attempt to balance the present and the past with an eye toward the future. We do the traditional prayers in the prayer book and the *Machzor*. We do each specific prescribed Torah reading and Haftarah on the same day as every traditional synagogue. Conservative Judaism presents a traditional model. What's different? We use a lot of English to help with understanding and we include everyone and even sit together. We absolutely respect the past but ensure that people can understand and that everyone can participate.

But the truth is, the sad truth is, that most of us have lost the sense of struggle, of weighing the past. We do anything we want. To those of you who don't understand why we have certain laws or rules, please, please, learn about the reasons for the laws you're questioning before you get so offended. No one is shunning anyone. But we are maintaining very important traditions.

Why are these laws so important?

To be Jewish is, first, to be a member of a *people*; we'll call it Jewishness. Second, it is to be a member of a *religion* called Judaism. The two dimensions, of Jewishness and Judaism, are completely intertwined. If you do not perpetuate Jewishness into the next generation of your family, it will mean that, after thousands of years, you will be the end of Judaism in your family. A movement of Judaism is not in the business of destroying Judaism by diluting it or blurring the lines; a Conservative Judaism's purpose is the perpetuation of Judaism. Every decision we make is towards that goal.

Let me say it really straight:
You and I are not going to be around all that long. We're just passing through. But we have a chance to be a part of something that goes back four thousand years. And four thousand years from today, Jewish people are going to be in services. Have respect for the continuum. Be a part of that continuum.

Now you thought that I finished the story of Uriah and Amos, because I told you how Amos died without ever coming home to his community. But I do have a postscript to the story. Amos' granddaughter was so moved by what her grandfather went through, and had so much respect for him and his tragedy, that she went and bought that farm. She bought the fields that he stared at in the dark. She reclaimed the inheritance, *her* inheritance.

That's exactly what Conservative Jews need to do.

Don't leave the fields for those who treat half of us as second-class citizens. Don't let them own Judaism because we don't live up to our obligations. Don't give in to a movement that, like the Amish, puts the details of the past over everything else.

And on the other hand, don't be so arrogant, and so superior that you simply throw the past away.

Do you really think you have all the answers?
Are you that full of pride in yourself?

Live in the present but for God's sake have respect for the past.

To belong to a Conservative synagogue means to have respect for the past. That's a great start. You are being true to your inheritance. Now it's not easy to find a way to be true to the beauty and meaning of the past and true to the beauty and meaning of the present. But that's okay: Anything worth anything is worth a struggle. The dream of every Conservative synagogue is to create a community of people who struggle together. To find a way to balance the past and the present is very difficult. But it's the only way to live.

I want you to be like Amos' granddaughter. She now owns the fields. She uses modern equipment to plow them. And she wears whatever she wants to wear.

As she walks those fields, she keeps her grandfather alive.

She walks beside all of her ancestors who worked those fields for centuries.

As she walks those fields, she knows who she is.

Chapter Seven
Jewish Lumberjacks and Jewish Planters

There is a tiny island in the middle of the Pacific Ocean, 2300 miles west of Chile, thousands of miles east of Australia. On April 5, 1772, which was Easter on the Christian calendar that year, a Dutch explorer who had been traveling for 17 days discovered this tiny island in the middle of nowhere. He called it Easter Island.

The island was deserted and wasted but there were around 400 huge stone statues, some of them as tall as a modern five-story building, weighing as much as 270 tons. Who carved these statues? How did they transport and raise such huge stone masses without cranes or even wheels? And after all that great effort, why did they throw all of the statues down?

Archaeologists eventually concluded that Polynesians settled the island eight hundred years before the Dutch explorer.

The island was created by a volcano and had very good, rich soil. The people lived there for hundreds of years, a happy and healthy society. They had a wonderful climate and rich natural resources such as fertile forests.

But after a few hundred years of peace and prosperity, the islanders started making thousands of huge statues. Why were they so obsessed with making these idols? They had plenty of food and didn't need to worry about survival. But people have a need to compete, and the twelve clans expressed their competitive spirit by vying to make the best idols. They had always used wood for many things, such as housing and boats. They also used wood to make lots of thick long ropes, made out of tree bark, by which 50-500 people could drag statues weighing 10 to 90 tons. But now they used even more trees for their mammoth statues.

Soon, they had used up all the trees. Without the trees, when it rained, the topsoil washed into the ocean. Without top soil, the crops died out. Since the people didn't have any wood, they couldn't make boats to fish. And they couldn't make escape boats, so they were stuck on the island. Since there was little food, the islanders started killing each other over what was left. Soon they became cannibals.

They started to think about it: They did not have enemies who killed them. No one had abandoned them. The climate hadn't changed. They had done it to themselves. The islanders realized that their idolatry had destroyed them. And so they went and toppled those statues; they threw them all down. But it was too late. And in 1860, the time of our American Civil War, some traders came and captured the survivors and sold them as slaves.

What were they thinking, those lumberjacks of Easter Island? What did they think was going to happen to them without their trees?

Now, think about another tiny island in the middle of a huge sea. There is a tiny island in the middle of space. It is many millions of miles from the nearest planet. It's called Earth.

In his best-selling book *Collapse: How Societies Choose to Fail or Succeed*, the geographer Jared Diamond points to the chilling possible parallel of Easter Island to Earth in modern times. Thanks to globalization, all countries on earth today share resources and affect each other, just like Easter Island's twelve clans. Earth is as isolated in space as Easter Island was in the Pacific Ocean. When the Easter Islanders got into difficulties, there was nowhere to which they could flee; no one to turn to for help. We modern earthlings will have no recourse if our troubles increase.

If you take a pessimistic point of view, the lesson of Easter Island is: If a few thousand islanders could ruin their island with stone tools and muscle power, how much the worse will it be as billions of people with metal and machine power destroy their environment?

But there is reason for cautious optimism: If we can ruin our earth, perhaps, if we care to do so, we can solve some of the problems we've caused. The earth was a beautiful island, a paradise, and we can return it to that state, if we begin to act.

For example, we have the knowledge and the resources to tackle the global warming problem and it would be irresponsible to delay when we know what we have to do. A swiftly changing climate plus human pressures on the landscape will mean disruption and damage. If we act responsibly, we will follow simple, practical solutions to slow down global warming and to respond to the changes coming our way.

But we're not interested in the issue. While Al Gore has made an effective film called *An Inconvenient Truth*, many have laughed him away as a greenie. Global warming is not a joke. But we only react to emergencies, and we don't get the urgency yet. The problem is that by the time we do get the emergency, it may be too late to do anything.

Why are we doing this to our earth? The problem is that we are busy making statues, the results of our competitive greed for financial gain. Our idol is money.

Let me tell you a Jewish story about idols. If I were to stop one hundred people on the street and ask them to tell me something about Abraham, they'd probably say that he was the first to believe in one God. If I were to ask a Jewish person to tell me two stories about Abraham that are in the Bible, they'd probably tell me that he took Isaac on the mountain to sacrifice him, and that when he was a boy he knocked down his father's idols. The story about the idols is not in the Bible, but it is a very famous *midrash*, a famous rabbinic legend. The story is that Abraham's father made idols in his idol shop. His father left him in charge one day. Abraham looked at the idols and decided that it was ridiculous to worship things that are made out of wood. He took an axe and chopped them into pieces. He left one big idol intact and put the axe in his arms. When his father came home, Abraham said, "The big idol did it." When his father said that this was ridiculous, that no idol could have destroyed the other idols, Abraham asked his father why he made a living from selling such pieces for people to worship.

Abraham's father's idol was not the piece of stone; he knew better than to worship something that he had made. Abraham's father's idol was money. Abraham's challenge was not just a religious one but also a moral one: How can you make your living doing something that you don't believe in?

This famous story is not based on anything in the Book of Genesis but on the later books of Second Isaiah and Daniel. The Midrash portrays Abraham as the first iconoclast, the first idol-smasher, the model Jewish person who questions everything and thinks freely and independently.

Ever since, we've been knocking down idols. Why do you think there have been so many Jewish Nobel Prize winners? Because we're always willing to think about a problem without assumptions.

Since Jewish people were the first idol-smashers, the story of Easter Island, a land that destroyed itself by making idols, should boggle our minds.

And yet, we Jewish people often build idols, don't we? We're so consumed with material consumption and so busy trying to turn ourselves into the American idol of financial success that we cut down every tree in sight.

So we allow those who would ruin nature for financial profit to do whatever they want.

We don't actively support those who are fighting to save and improve our environment. We don't even recycle; we can't be bothered. If there's an oil crisis, we use more gas than ever before. We want what we want when we want it. Who cares about the earth?

God does. And Judaism, as usual, was way ahead of modern trends and even has a holiday about the environment. On Tu B'shvat, the fifteenth day of the Hebrew month of Shevat, we celebrate another New Year's Festival, the New Year for Trees. We actually have a holiday about trees because we know, as opposed to the people of Easter Island, that trees are necessary for our survival and that trees symbolize the resources of our lives. Judaism creates a different kind of environment for us, providing every resource we need in order to live a happy and meaningful life.

So let me tell you about some of the trees, some of the festivals in our forest. Yom Kippur is the most important Jewish holiday, and second to it is Shabbat; every Sabbath is more important than Rosh Hashanah. The Sabbath is for reflection, for the opportunity to break out of our routines. On Shabbat, you cannot use money; that in itself liberates us from the idol of money. After Rosh Hashanah, there are three festivals, all equal in importance on the next level down. Passover is for thinking about the poor and the homeless and the fact that we are free. A second festival is Sukkot the Harvest festival; it is for thanksgiving, when we think about everything that we've received from nature and our environment. There is also Shavu'ot, the Festival of First Fruits, when we celebrate the best things in our lives, the *bikkurim*, and the revelation of the Ten Commandments on Mt. Sinai. And one of these commandments says that you should not worship idols that you have made.

So we have this Jewish environment with all of these resources. And yet, we destroy these resources and are left, on an island, by ourselves, trying to figure out how to survive emotionally.

We have rituals for every aspect of the life cycle, including mourning for our loved ones who have passed on. Judaism knows that when we are confronted with an anniversary of a death, a *yahrzeit*, we have an especially tough and sad time. And we feel all alone on an island without trees. And so Judaism gives us something to do. We come and say the Mourner's Kaddish at shul with other people who are doing the same thing. This is a precious and thoughtful resource but most of us do not make use of it, even though it would help us with a tough time

We keep cutting down the trees on our island.
We don't use the rituals of comfort.

We don't observe the Sabbath or the holidays.
We don't concretize the idea that life is a cycle.
We forget to help the poor as Passover teaches.
Or to enjoy the years of Harvest as Sukkot teaches.
And the moral reinforcement that Shavuot presents.
And we miss important and basic reinforcements for living. We don't understand who we are.

So who are we? Judaism believes that you have a soul and that your soul is eternal. You, the real you, the essence of you, will never die.

If so, what is your body? The environment for your soul. Now you could say, "Okay, since my soul is the real me, I don't have to take care of my body." But Judaism takes the opposite view: just as you must take care of the earth God gave us, so we must take care of the bodies God gave us, our immediate environments. Many of us understand this and on a regular if not daily basis work hard to maintain our physical health. To those of you who work at it, and it is work, it's hard grueling work that takes great discipline, to those who have made exercise a part of your lives, understand that you are obeying the commandments of God.

To those of you who do not exercise, understand loud and clear that you are like a lumberjack on Easter Island or like someone who pollutes the environment, cutting down more trees every year. We know so much about the benefits of physical exercise. We know that no matter how old you are or what shape you're in, you will benefit greatly from physical exertion. There are simply no excuses. Up until last year, I sadly admit that I was the king of excuses. There's no excuse you can give that I haven't used. It was Mark Twain who originally quipped, "If I had known that I was going to live that long, I would have taken better care of myself!" That's cute but it's nonsense. Judaism teaches us discipline through ritual so that we can use discipline to improve our lives in every way, physically, morally, spiritually. In the coming year, if you have not been working at improving your physical self, you simply must. It's not up to anyone else. No excuses.

Because, you see, there is a tiny island in the middle of earth's humanity. It's you. You rarely admit it to anyone, not even to yourself, but you often feel lonely. You can have a life filled with people in which you are rarely alone, but feel loneliness all the same, loneliness for someone who shares your interests, loneliness for someone on your intellectual or emotional level, the loneliness for someone who really understands you.

John Donne might have said no man is an island, but that was pretty, wishful thinking about the human condition. A lot of us *are* islands, entire to ourselves, as alone as Easter Island in the middle of the Pacific Ocean or Earth in the middle of space.

And yet, instead of planting trees on our islands, we cut trees down.

We have natural resources. But we squander them. We have brains. We have families, we have a community; we have a religion.

And yet:
We don't use our brains very much.
We're angry with this one and that one in our family.
We absent ourselves from our community;
And we never really understood much about our religion to begin with.
We cut out a person in our life, a relative or a friend, and we cut another tree down.

I mentioned the film *An Inconvenient Truth*, which details how we negatively affect our environment. Here are a few other inconvenient truths:

You are wrecking the Jewish environment of your life.
It's inconvenient to be Jewish.
It's inconvenient to be different.
It's inconvenient to stop and observe rituals.
It's inconvenient to pay honor to your loved ones who have passed on.
It's inconvenient to be involved in the political process to save the earth from greed.
It's inconvenient to work out and sweat to make yourself healthier.

But the truth is that all of this is who you are and who you should be, and part of your loneliness comes from your failure to be true to yourself.

In order to make idols, we destroy our Jewish resources.

And we are more and more isolated, and our environment is wasted. We keep cutting down one tree after another to make one idol after another.

For many of us, there is nothing Jewish about our environment. Those Jewish resources have led to our people's miraculous survival for four thousand years but we are quite content to cut down those trees.

We must realize that we need all of the holidays and rituals which foster community. And we need community.

My favorite example about a sense of community comes from an unusual source, the life of Johnny Appleseed. Most of us know that he was a real person named John Chapman who was born around the time of the American Revolution. John Chapman lived in the first half-century of the history of the United States (1774-1845). Until recently, I had an image of Johnny Appleseed as a solitary man, a man who "walked alone," who walked across part of America dropping apple seeds where he went. I don't know where I got that image; maybe from an old Disney show. But the truth is that Johnny Appleseed didn't just plant apple trees here and there at random. He planted orchards; communities of trees, in key places where he thought people would live. He either came with people to their new towns or he was one step ahead of where he knew people were soon going to be living. And then every year he would return to the nurseries he had created to tend and prune and care for his trees.

This man who never married or had children played a role in his society. He didn't plant one tree here or there but orchards, communities of trees. Johnny Appleseed believed in God, not in idols like the people of Easter Island. He didn't cut down trees; he spent his life planting them.

Johnny Appleseed knew that you can be single but a part of things; even this loner showed how one of the basic elements in nature, the tree, cannot stand alone but should be planted as a part of a community.

The climate didn't change on Easter Island; they did it to themselves.

Our climate hasn't changed; Judaism is still here. Remember that societies collapse when they destroy their resources. So do people. We are often on the edge of collapse.

But it doesn't have to be this way. The Jewish community is an orchard, filled with precious resources that are natural resources to nourish you, resources that exist for your happiness.

So the choice is clear: You can knock down trees or you can plant them. You can be a Jewish lumberjack, cutting down the trees on your island, or you can be a Jewish Johnny Appleseed, planting communities of trees.

You may live in a nice community and you may not appreciate what you have; a community with nice people who care about each other. But you can't feel community if you're out there, planting one tree here and one tree there, all by yourself. No one will see those trees you've planted. The secret location of those trees will die with you.

Johnny Appleseed understood that you have to plant your trees; you have to be engaged in the activities of your life, in the community, so that all may appreciate your efforts and benefit from them. When you attend services for a minyan or a Shabbat or a holiday, you plant a tree. You plant a tree when you say hello and start a conversation with someone you didn't know.

When I went to Israel with a group, we went and planted trees in a Jewish National Fund forest. Our task was to plant trees where there was nothing, a barren hill of dirt and rock. Each of us dedicated a tree for a loved one or in memory of someone. I was busy planting my tree for my own reasons. But when I finished, I looked around, and we'd planted a small community of trees, and I looked around again, and I saw a beautiful forest that would grow and flourish for years and years to come. That was really something.

Chapter Eight

When They Burned Down My Father's Shul
or
Do You Have Any Enemies?

When I was six years old, my mother gave birth to twins and my family moved to a bigger house closer to my father's synagogue. It was hard to say goodbye to my friends on the block but even harder to make friends in my new neighborhood. There were lots of kids around; our block was across the street from the huge elementary school I would begin to attend a couple of weeks after the move. The problem was that all of the kids had organized a club that had as its sole purpose hating the new kid on the block. When I asked one of them about it, he said that it wasn't up to him, that that was the club. I persisted and asked him if we could be friends. He said he'd think about it. He thought about it and became my best friend. But two of the other kids on the block, Ronnie Fry and Joey Dalbey[1], continued to hate me. One day after school, they shoved me around, and when by the next day nothing had happened, they beat me up, with one holding me down and the other one punching me over and over again. I was six years old and terrified. I told my parents who said I should report it to my teacher the next day. I did, but she said that since it had not happened in class, it was not her problem. When they beat me up again the next day, my mother went to the principal who said that it was after school and it was not her problem. When they beat me up again the day after that, and I came home bleeding, my father called Mr. Dalbey. My father explained that he was Rabbi Scolnic and that he wanted to talk to him about a problem between our boys, that Joey and his friend Ronnie were beating me up every day. When my father got off the phone, I saw a look on his face I'd never seen before. He went upstairs and came back with a pillow and told me to punch it. That day, my father the rabbi taught me how to fight.

I didn't understand what was going on.

"I don't hate these kids, Daddy," I said. "Why do they hate me?"
"Sometimes," my father said, "People choose to be our enemies. When they do, we have to know that we *have* enemies."

My father didn't tell me what Mr. Dalbey had said to him, which I later found out went something like this:

[1] Not their real names.

"So let me get this straight, Rabbi. You're telling me how to raise my boy? You people never know when to quit."

My father also didn't tell me that when he was growing up in Fort Worth, Texas, he was the object of both verbal and physical abuse from some of the other kids who hated him for being Jewish.

After my punching lesson, my father said, "Try one more time. Tell the young Dalbey that you'd like to be his friend. If it doesn't work, be ready."

So the next day in recess, I told Joey Dalbey that I'd like to be his friend. He said, "Sure, I'll be your friend." I was very happy until another kid told me what Joey was telling everyone he was going to do. He was going to knock on my door that afternoon after school, and when I came out, he was going to beat me up right on my front lawn.

So I was ready. When he came knocking, I burst out of the door and before he could do a thing, I started punching. He ran away. Neither Joey nor Ronnie ever touched me again. Neither of them ever spoke to me again during all the years of elementary school, even though we were usually in the same class. That was fine with me; I didn't need them to be my friends. I just needed them to leave me alone.

Years passed. I'm walking in the morning to junior high, and I see a lot of police cars across the street at the elementary school. It turns out that a group of junior high kids had broken in and vandalized the school the night before. They had poured glue on the piano wires, destroyed furniture and painted horrible words on the walls. Among those kids were none other than Joey Dalbey and Ronnie Fry. They were just kids, the authorities said, so they got off without punishment. They walked around the junior high with big smiles like they'd gotten away with murder.

One day, about a year later, I passed by them, and they stopped talking. When I walked away, they started talking again.

A few weeks later, on the first night of Pesach, my father got a call from the police in the middle of the night. Our synagogue was on fire. The firemen stopped the blaze before it spread to the sanctuary, but one wing, including the library and my father's office, was destroyed.

I went with him the next morning. To this day, I can still see my father's face. I can still see all of our Jewish books reduced to ashes.

Eventually, the police caught those who had done it, a group of neighborhood teenagers that included Joey Dalbey and Ronnie Fry.

I tell you this story because many of us are like me when I was six. We cannot comprehend why anyone would hate us. We are so good; we are so innocent. We think that we can reason and negotiate and make friends with anyone.

But my father had it exactly right: The person who chooses to be your enemy *is* your enemy, no matter what you think.

People, for no reason at all, may choose to hate us and to act on that hatred. When they do, we must know that we have enemies.

Once you wake up to that fact, you ask: "What should we do about it?" This is the question of our time. When you fight back, what will the consequences be?

By punching Joey Dalbey, did I start a chain of events that led to my synagogue getting burned? I don't want to think that way, but it's possible. But what else should I have done?
Should I have allowed myself to live in fear?
Should I just have been a passive victim?
Did my father contribute to the arson by calling Mr. Dalbey?
But he was just trying to reason with another father.

My family and I tried every other route before fighting back. Whom do I blame for that synagogue fire? I blame parents who raised their children to hate. And I blame the authorities that didn't punish those delinquents when they vandalized the elementary school and were allowed to get away with it.

Evil people must be punished before they do something worse.
Evil, on whatever level, must be countered with strength.
First you try every other route; then you fight.

Israel has tried every other route, giving land for peace and land in exchange for nothing at all in unilateral withdrawals from Gaza and Lebanon. The response has only been more violence.

Should Israel let the rockets fall on its people?
Should Israel let its soldiers get kidnapped?
Should Israel let its children on their way to school be blown up on buses?
What exactly do you want Israel to do?

First you have to understand that you have enemies; then you have to decide what to do. We have to figure this out and it's morally complex.

Our enemies fight in the most barbaric and uncivilized fashion and we are still trying to fight like civilized human beings. They don't fight fair and we're trying to fight by the rules.

My father was right: Try everything you can think of before you fight. Try different tactics. Talk to the teacher. Talk to the principal. But we can't talk to the principal of what is supposed to be the world's school because the corrupt farce called the United Nations simply does not care about Jewish lives and doesn't say a thing when we get killed.

The difference between our enemies and us is clear:
Osama bin Laden said that he loves death but America loves life.

Moses said: "Behold, you have before you life and death. Choose life."

We do choose life. And since we love life, we have to fight the forces of death. In the process, we will have to take lives. That's what happens in a war: People die. And we can't stand it.

We can't stand it when Hezbollah cowards shoot missiles from backyards so that families will get killed when Israel responds in self-defense.
We can't stand it when we see the death tolls.
We can't stand fighting their fire with our fire.

In my community, I know a lot of nice people. After all of these years, I can say that there isn't a person in the community who, given a situation, I couldn't sit down and talk to. We might disagree, but we could talk about it.

What's that old song by Dave Mason?

> *So let's leave it alone*
> *'Cause we can't see eye to eye*
> *There ain't no good guy*
> *There ain't no bad guy*
> *There's just you and me*
> *And we just disagree.*

If we talked, we'd either get somewhere, or we'd leave it alone; we'd agree to disagree.

But the world isn't like a congregation of nice people. There are millions upon millions of people who, like Joey Dalbey and Ronnie Fry, are raised to hate. And make no mistake: they hate you.

They say, out loud, "We want to destroy Israel; we want to kill all Jews everywhere."
So let me ask you: What part of "We want to destroy Israel, we want to kill all Jews everywhere" don't you understand?

But we don't get it; we think it will stop.

We're like Charlie Brown. Linus asks Charlie Brown: "If you have some problem in your life, do you believe you should try to solve it right away or think about it for a while?"
Charlie Brown replies: "I believe you should think about it for a while ..."
Linus asks: "To give yourself time to do the right thing about the problem?"
And Charlie replies, "No, to give it time to go away."

That's what we want; we want these problems to go away.

But the problem of radical Muslim hatred is not going to go away.

Let me tell you a story from the life of a friend, Dr. Israel Dvoretsky. He volunteered to serve in a medical clinic in Gaza, treating Arabs. He wanted to build bridges, to show the Arabs that Israelis want to live in peace and help them. Every day, when he came into work, there would be a cup of coffee on his desk, brought by his Arab assistant. At one point, the assistant asked if the doctor would visit his sick mother, who lived in a refugee camp. Israelis had been warned that it was extremely dangerous to go to that camp. But Israel went twice, out of affection for his assistant, and healed the mother. When Israel came to the clinic on his last day, there was no cup of coffee. He asked his assistant, who replied that he would not get it. When Israel asked why, the assistant said, "Because I hate you. I've always hated you. And if I could kill you, I would."

Picture our friend Israel as the nation of Israel. It doesn't matter what Israel does right; the enemies still hate.

We have enemies, and we have to know it.

Another friend, Dr. Edward Kaplan of Yale has shown, through statistical study of thousands of Europeans, that the harsher one's view is of Israel the

65

likelier one is to be an anti-Semite. Most of the people who hold the most negative views of Israel think that Jewish people engage in shady financial practices and have too much business power.

Criticizing Israel is politically correct but being openly anti-Jewish, as Mel Gibson could tell you, is often not worth the hassle. Just for the record, many people told me that I was wrong when I insisted that *The Passion of the Christ* was horrendously anti-Semitic.

Now if to be anti-Israel is a way of being anti-Jewish, shouldn't Jewish people think twice before publicly criticizing Israel?

When I was six, playing imaginary war games with my friends, one of them would ask me to cover him while he crawled behind the swing set.

When Jewish people criticize Israel, we provide *cover* for anti-Semites. They say, "Look at those ads in the New York Times with all of those Jewish names denouncing Israel. If they can do it, so can we."

Is that what we want to do, provide cover for anti-Jewish hatred?

We who do not risk our lives every day;
Who don't send our children into harm's way;
Who don't spend endless hours in bomb shelters;
Who don't worry about the next rocket barrage;
How dare we tell the Israelis how and when to negotiate or fight?

We should stop taking self-righteous potshots at a people who are fighting our fight for Jewish survival. The very least we can do is keep quiet when we have questions about Israel's actions.

The whole world jumps all over Israel on the basis of a doctored photograph or a scene that's staged. Do we American Jews have to join the piling-on? Do we have to hold Israel down while everybody else is punching her?

If I am not for myself, who will be for me?
If the Jewish people don't support Israel, who will?
All that Israel wants to do is live in peace.

Why should we criticize that?

And if Israel makes a mistake, it will be honest and explain. Israel is intensely self-critical. We can depend on Israel telling the truth. We don't need to say anything.

When They Burned Down My Father's Shul or Do You Have Any Enemies?

Ask yourself the simple question: Why is there so much attention on Israel and Jewish people? Muslims are killing hundreds of thousands of people right now in Darfur, and the world is quiet. Let Israel kill one Muslim in self-defense and the world screams. Israel is a tiny land. We are a tiny people, 14 million out of 7 billion on this earth. Why so much hatred?

The answer is that Israel and the Jewish people represent the foundations of Western civilization, and the Islamic Jihad wants to destroy those foundations *because* their own religion is based on Judaism.

It goes back fourteen hundred years to a man named Muhammad who wanted to develop a belief in One God that would incorporate Judaism and Christianity. He called it Islam, meaning "submission". Muhammad wanted everyone to live in submission to the Will of God as he understood it. He assumed that the Jewish tribes of Arabia would submit to his great vision. When Muhammad realized that the Arabian Jews would not join him, he developed an intense hatred and conducted murderous attacks, assassinating Jewish individuals, destroying Jewish communities by expulsion, enslavement and massacre. In the case of the Khaybar Jews, Muhammad had the male leadership killed. Do you remember the name of the rockets that flew down on northern Israel this summer? Khaybar-1 rockets, named for the place of Muhammad's famous massacre of the Jews.

So when we speak of Islamic fundamentalists, we are correct because they derive their hatred and violence straight from Muhammad. They derive their inspiration from chapters, called Suras, 5 and 9 of the Koran. Read the words of Muhammad about what his followers should do to those who will not submit to Islam. You won't be able to sleep that night.

Now other religions, including Judaism, have chapters of their sacred texts that are morally problematic. But we have evolved and do not follow those chapters. Islamic fundamentalists take the worst parts of the Koran as the basis for their horrible violence. They want Shariah, Islamic law, with its repressive tyranny and its regressive discrimination against women, to be the law of the world.

But it's even worse. One of the scariest moments of my life was when I read about the concept of Dar al-Islam. In this basic Muslim view, there are two parts of the world: The part that is *already* Muslim, and the part that is *not yet* Muslim. If there is a land that was once ruled by Muslims, it cannot pass out of Muslim hands. So the existence of Israel is abhorrent because it should be Muslim. The goal is the destruction of Israel. Israel must defend itself. And we must support Israel.

There's a line at the end of *Harry Potter and the Goblet of Fire*, when the wise old wizard says that a time is coming when we will have to choose between what is right and what is easy.

It's easy to close your eyes.
It's easy to be Charlie Brown and think it's all going to go away.
It's easy to live your life in the relative security of America.
It's easy to pretend there isn't a war going on in this world.
It's easy not to think about 9/11.

And we nice people, who don't think we have an enemy in the world, who think that people will be nice to us if we just treat them nicely, better wake up.

We have to look at the big picture.

We have to see more than our current battles; we have to see the larger war against civilization. Islam means submission. Jihadists use terror to scare the world to surrender and are succeeding in Europe. We must not submit.

We can argue over tactics, about when and where to fight, over security measures, about how to develop better intelligence.

All these discussions are necessary because we're just feeling our way into a new war with an enemy that doesn't play by any rules at all.

This is all really, really hard to figure out. Learning how to play a game like chess means to learn the rules. But we're facing an opponent who doesn't follow one of those rules and is happily willing to sacrifice every one of its pieces and blow up the whole board.

We are just beginning to learn how to counter this kind of violence.

And so we will make terrible, tragic mistakes. Our political leaders will think that they know what to do and sometimes they will be right and successful. Sometimes they will be right but unsuccessful. Other times, they will think they're doing what's right but create a situation that's even worse than before and then no one will know what to do.
They will make huge mistakes out of arrogance, thinking that they know what to do when they don't.

They will lose focus and try to do too much too fast.

We have to be totally honest about our mistakes. But even with all the problems, America is the only major force in the war to protect civilization.

When They Burned Down My Father's Shul or Do You Have Any Enemies?

So do we have to be so angry at each other? This country is terribly divided between the screaming voices on the left and the screaming voices on the right, each side pushing an agenda that is only an educated guess.

American anguish about the two wars that are raging in Iraq, the sectarian civil war and the rebellion against a democratically-elected government, has led to endless finger-pointing about lies from one side and treason from the other. We've turned other Americans into the bad guys because we can't see eye-to-eye. It's very easy to scream and blame. It's harder to find a new solution, such as breaking the artificial state called Iraq back into its three natural parts and/our redeploying our troops.

When everybody's screaming, nothing gets done and nothing changes.

But no matter what, we should not argue about America's need to actively defend our way of life.
And we should certainly not argue about Israel's need to defend its people.

We must not be divided; we must be united.
We must not appease evil. We must be strong.

I believe, deep in my heart, that war is the most horrible thing in the world. I am so non-violent that my fight with Joey Dalbey at the age of six was one of a very few physical confrontations in my whole life.

But I learned some lessons from that fight.
People hate you for no reason at all.
Whether you like it or not, you have enemies.
They hurt you.
They don't fight fairly; they don't follow any rules.

And you try different ways to stop them without fighting back.
But you find out that no one cares about you except your own.
And you learn that sometimes, even though it's the hardest thing in the world for you to do, you have to fight.

It's not a matter of choosing between what is right and what is wrong.
We have to choose between what is right and what is easy.

In this world, there is no easy.

We have to do what's right.

Chapter Nine
Which Child Are You?
or
King of the Mountain

At a Passover Seder, at the ritual meal that we observe on the first two nights of Pesach, one of the most famous passages in the Haggadah concerns the Four Sons.

One is called the *hacham*, the Wise Child. He asks an intelligent and informed question about the Passover Seder.

One is called the *rasha*, the Rebellious Child. He asks an antagonistic question, showing his disdain for Judaism and its rituals.

A third is called the *tam*, the Simple Child, and he asks a question on a very basic level.

And then there is the child who is so young that he doesn't even know how to ask a question at all.

I use this text from Passover in order to ask you a question: Which child are *you*?

Are you the Wise Child, who constantly learns more and more about Judaism?
Are you the Rebellious Child, always eager to show that you don't buy any of this Jewish stuff and that you would never think about learning anything about it?
Are you the Simple Child who stopped learning when you were a child, who doesn't know anything more than you did at thirteen years old?
Or do you know so little that you don't even know what question to ask first?

Which child are you?

After twenty-seven years as a rabbi, I know enough about American Jewish people to generalize: Most of us are in the third group.

Yes, some of us are Wise Children who read Jewish books, attend adult education classes and services and stay current on events affecting Judaism and Israel.

And of course, some of us are Rebellious Children and don't want to have much to do with the whole thing but do identify themselves as Jewish and who therefore come to the Seder table and a few High Holiday services but that's really it.

Still, most of us are in the third group. We don't learn or participate very much but also have only goodwill towards Judaism and the Jewish people. Educationally speaking, we know less than we did when we were children. One of the problems is that what we *do* know is what we were taught when we were kids. And so we think about Judaism as something for children.

When we were kids, we were taught in a certain way so that we would receive a foundation of values. Children should have heroes who embody great values. Children should learn a strong sense of good and evil and right and wrong. Jewish children should learn their Bible stories so that they will have a strong moral and ethical and religious foundation for their lives.

But in the process, our teachers, in both secular and religious schools, need to leave certain aspects of the truth out of the picture. In a way, it's too bad, because the truth is usually more interesting than the idealized version presented to children. That's okay, as long as the children grow up and learn the truth when they're older. The problem comes when we never learn the truth later on and never gain the understanding that the truth could give us.

So I'm going to teach you something here that I bet you don't know about American history on an adult level, and then I'm going to teach you something that I bet you don't know about Judaism on the same issue on an adult level, and then I'm going to tell you what I think an adult understanding on this topic can mean to our lives. And I'm going to try to show you how being a *hacham*, a wise child who asks questions and learns, is better than remaining a *tam*, a simple adult who never moves beyond a child's understanding.

All of us, when we were children, learned about the American Revolution. We learned that great men, like Patrick Henry, roused their generation to a courageous rebellion against tyranny.

All of us can repeat one of the most famous lines in American history, "Give me liberty or give me death!" We picture Patrick Henry rising in the Virginia Convention and defiantly risking his life. We read the speech he gave, filled with references to the British tyrants and how they have enslaved the Colonial Americans. Since they live under this slavery, they have no choice but to rise up and make war against the tyrants.

I started to wonder why Patrick Henry would speak about slavery. Taxation without representation is unfair, I agree, but it's not *slavery*. Slavery means that one person owns, literally owns another human being and controls everything he or she does.

So I began to read adult books about early American history. I quickly realized that I had been simple, that I had always had a child's understanding of Patrick Henry and that famous speech. First, I found that Patrick Henry never spoke the words attributed to him. Other people wrote that speech long after he was dead. They wrote those words decades later when slavery had become *the* issue in American debate.

Second, I found that Patrick Henry had risen that famous day out of fear of the British not because they were enslaving anyone but because they wanted to *free* the slaves of people like Patrick Henry. He was ready to go to war to stop the British from fleeing his slaves. Give me liberty or give me death? More like, "Give me the freedom to enslave others or give me death!"

One of the generally unknown stories about the American Revolution is that the British offered freedom to all slaves who would join their side and that a huge number of slaves ran away from their white masters to find freedom with the British. Between 80,000 and 100,000 slaves left their plantations during the war. One was Ralph Henry, owned by Patrick Henry. Another was Henry Washington, slave of George Washington. Thirty slaves ran away from Thomas Jefferson's Monticello. *Two-thirds* of the slaves in South Carolina ran away.[1]

Give me liberty or give me death? Tens of thousands of slaves ran away to gain their liberty.

Even as a child, I always knew that the Founding Fathers of my beloved America were slave-owners. But I thought that in their time, everyone accepted slavery as moral. Now I learned that the supposedly evil British had exposed the hypocrisy of people who shouted about liberty while owning other people, that the British freed tens of thousands of slaves almost a century *before* Abraham Lincoln. Slavery was not considered moral by the British and was not accepted as a fact of life by the slaves themselves.

[1] If you saw Mel Gibson's movie fantasy *The Patriot*, you saw a fictionalized version of Francis Marion, the famous Swamp Fox. In the movie, Gibson's black slaves follow their master into the fight for freedom. But in real history, at least one of Francis Marion's slaves ran away and fought with the mounted Black Dragoons against Francis Marion.

Colonel Patrick Henry of the First Virginia Regiment went so far as to order patrols to keep Virginia slaves from accepting the British offer of freedom to those who would join their side. Henry knew the moral contradiction and explicitly admitted that slavery was horrible. He asked, "Would anyone believe I am the master of slaves of my own purchase?" But he was willing to fight to the *death* to keep his slaves.

It makes me look at the American Revolution itself very differently when I think that one of the causes of the war was the fervent desire to perpetuate slavery.

I am a patriotic American. I love this country with all my heart. But I'm not a kid anymore, and I have to understand things on an adult level. I have to be the Wise Child who says, "Why were our Founding Fathers on the *wrong* side of this important human and moral issue?"

Our country was built on an immoral foundation that would tear the nation apart and would only be resolved by another, even bloodier conflict, the Civil War. The decision to keep slaves in the face of moral wrong nearly did this country in.

If we're going to understand America, we have to understand its past.

I hope that this example will indicate that education should never end. Since we should approach Judaism as adults, I'll turn to a parallel example from the Book of Genesis, one that affects us as Jewish people. You'll remember the story of Joseph. His brothers sell Joseph into slavery because they are jealous of his standing with their father Jacob, who indicated that Joseph would be his heir by giving him a coat of many colors. Joseph rises from slavery to become the Number Two Man in Egypt. He interprets Pharaoh's dream to mean that there will be seven years of plenty and then seven years of famine. Joseph is given the power to control the economy. So during the seven years of plenty, he puts the surplus away and grows huge herds of livestock so that there will be enough food for the country during the years of famine.

When I was a child, I pictured the Egyptians lining up to receive food from the reserves created by Joseph's wisdom and foresight.

But now as an adult, I read the Book of Genesis with open eyes. The Bible is a very adult book that tells the truths we *don't* want to hear.

So what does the Bible actually say? That at first, when the Egyptians lined up for food, Joseph gave freely to all of the hungry Egyptians.[2]

But the famine continued into the next year, and the Egyptians bought every-thing they could until their money ran out.[3]

And when the famine continued into the third year, the Egyptians still needed food, and they bought it with all of their livestock.[4]

And then when they came back again for food, they came to Joseph with a new proposition, that they would sell their land to Pharaoh and become his serfs. The deal was that they would give Pharaoh 20% of their produce and keep 80% for themselves. Joseph accepted this, and so most of the farmland in Egypt now belonged to Pharaoh.[5]

All of this was legal and ethical. But on a higher plane, it was taking advan-tage of those who were hungry and needy, leaving them without anything that belonged to them. And when the famine was over, the Egyptians didn't re-member that it was their idea. All they knew was that they had nothing. After Joseph died, there arose not only a new Pharaoh but also a new dynasty. While Joseph may have been part of a dynasty that was Semitic in origin, the new dynasty was made up of native Egyptians.

There was terrible resentment of the man who had caused the Egyptians to lose their land. And so what did the new native Egyptian dynasty do? They enslaved the Israelites; they made *them* serfs.

What goes around, come around.

Now it's true that unlike Patrick Henry or George Washington or Thomas Jefferson, Joseph did not personally gain from his actions.

But just as American slavery did America in, so Joseph's enserfment of the Egyptians seems to have done the Israelites in.

What goes around comes around.

You will pay the price of immorality.

Whether you're the United States of America or Joseph, temporary political control does not mean moral right. Might does not make right.

[2] Genesis 41:56.
[3] Genesis 47:14.
[4] Genesis 47:16.
[5] Genesis 47:18-26.

Joseph started as the favored son and was thrown into the pit.
You would think that the experience of being a slave would have taught him not to enslave others.
Joseph had been sold into slavery; he responded by enserfing Egypt.
Do you see the cycle, the action and reactions?
Joseph had been a slave but he didn't get the point.

And so God made us all enslaved so that we would *all* get the point and never forget it.
We remember that we were slaves in Egypt, controlled by others. We never forget that experience. We know that we were not slaves in Egypt because of any lack or failure on our part. In fact, we may have been enslaved partly because Joseph was so successful as Vizier of Egypt that many of the native Egyptians became serfs to Joseph's Pharaoh and resented Joseph's skill in planning and organization. We may have been slaves in Egypt because we were so successful and other people resented it.

I've given you two examples of what adult learning, *hacham* learning is. It is telling the truth, not pediatric truth for the kids, but real-life history and the kind of hard-edged truths that the Bible, when you actually read it, gives us.

But let's ask a *rasha* question: What does this have to do with me? Why should I care about slavery, whether it's in early America or ancient Egypt?

There are many responses to this question, but the one I'm thinking about now is that both our Founding Fathers, and our father Joseph, failed to meet the test that I call "King of the Mountain." Did you play "King of the Mountain" when you were a kid? Through wrestling, shoving and pushing, you get to the top. And you say ""I'm King of the Mountain."

In real life, when you get to the top of the hill, it is as great a test as when you're at the bottom trying to get yourself together. When you're king of the hill, how are you going to treat the people who are below you? Will you meet the test of success?

Let me tell you two stories, both of which I heard from my archaeologist friends. There is a mild-mannered Archaeology Professor who investigates a mound in Syria and finds that it is a tell, a mound that has strata (levels), each of which contains the remains of one period of human occupation on that site. The professor is a kind person, very appreciative of those who help him in his effort. He gets a grant from a foundation and brings other experts to help him in the adventure. They work for years, season after season, and they are very successful. Eventually they identify the site and more money rolls in to back them. The archaeology professor becomes more and more famous.

One day he stands at the top of the mound, looking across the Syrian plain. And on top of that mound, he has a moment when all of the recent events of his life come rushing at him. He stands there and he is no longer just the head of an archaeological expedition but a king, the monarch of all he surveys. And from that moment on, he is an obnoxious, arrogant, self-centered person.

That's the first story. The second story is about a famous television actor one of my archaeologist friends met. Some of you will remember "Poldark," a great BBC television series about the adventures of a hero named Ross Poldark in 18th century Cornwall. The show ended thirty years ago but I still remember how it began with scenes of waves crashing against mighty cliffs. Poldark was played by a very handsome, quite dashing actor named Robin Ellis. My friend met Robin Ellis and his wife and asked Mrs. Ellis how they had met. And here was what Mrs. Ellis said: "I was doing Public Relations in New York and there was a huge black tie dinner at the Waldorf Astoria. Mr. Ellis needed a date, so I grabbed at the opportunity to sit next to him. I'd had a lot of contact with famous actors, and most of them were nasty, but I figured I could get a great photograph to show my friends out of the deal. And then, during the dinner, there was a disaster. The waiter poured hot coffee all over Robin Ellis, all over his tuxedo. I was ready for the usual horrible putdowns that I'd heard from so many famous people, only to hear Robin Ellis, his suit ruined at a dinner where he was the guest of honor, comforting and reassuring the waiter that it was all right, that it was an accident, that he would do nothing to get him fired, that he knew he felt badly and that he should just relax. At that very moment, I stopped having a crush on Poldark and fell in love with Robin Ellis. And I married him."

She married him because she had found a person who was not only successful but who had not let that success go to his head; he was still a wonderful human being.

How do you wear your success? How many people do you know who never had money growing up, now have made a lot, and are positively snobby about what they have? They stand at the top of the hill, the monarch of all they survey, and they forget that, not too long ago, they were slaves in Egypt.

I know quite a few people who were raised in humble surroundings in the Bronx and Brooklyn. I enjoy listening to people speak with pride about their humble beginnings and how they might not have had much money but had great values and wonderful families. They don't pretend that they sprang into life with a silver spoon in their mouths: they are happy to tell you where and what they come from. They were born in Egypt and came through the wilderness and now they're doing well, but they don't forget what slavery was like and they wear their success with some humor and humility.

We talk all the time about coping with failure. But we should also talk about coping with success. Many of us don't cope with success. We change and we lose who we were, we lose the best parts of ourselves. Every day, someone tells me a story about the way their boss or their superior lorded it over them. Every day, children tell me about successful parents who are impatient or critical about their lives.

This is not how it should be. When you go back to the earliest laws in the Bible, you find that the Torah is vitally concerned with two situations: What if someone is in control of you or what if you're in control of someone else? A primary reason for the commandment of the Sabbath day, the central ritual of our religion, is not only so *you* will rest but also so that the people *under* you should have a day off. The earliest Jewish laws speak concretely about not taking advantage of another's misfortune.

We must not take advantage of those who are in lower or subservient positions. Don't let your success go to your head. Your success, and their relative lack of success, may not be because you're so great and they're not, or because you worked so hard and they didn't. Don't be so full of yourself. Remember: What goes around comes around.

I began with the question of "Which child are you? Are you a *hacham*, a wise child who asks questions in order to learn and grow?" If so, now that you're an adult, learn as an adult.

I took two examples from the past. The first was from American history: I discussed how some of our Founding Fathers like Patrick Henry built America on the cracked, immoral foundation of slavery, only to see our country literally cut in two as a result. My second example was from the Bible: I discussed how the enslavement of the Israelites might have been caused by the actions of Joseph, who had been a slave himself but nevertheless enslaved the Egyptians.

What can we learn from these examples from the past about our lives? When you're *king* of the hill, like Patrick Henry or Joseph, you must not forget what life was like when you were at the *bottom* of the hill.

So for all who have a simple understanding of Judaism, understand this: We have a lot to learn from the truth.

Chapter Ten

A Letter to My Grandson

Dear Alexander Rubin Scolnic Dobin,

I'm reading you this letter on a special day, the day of your *b'rit milah*, your *bris*, your circumcision. Thank God, you won't remember today, but I will. It's the day when we gave you a name. It's the day when we brought you into the Covenant with God, the covenant our people have marked with every baby boy going back to the first baby boy, Isaac, son of Abraham. Since this is not an easy day for you, as I read you this letter, you may fall asleep. Don't feel bad; people have been sleeping through my speaking for many years now. In your case, I'm only too happy to help your parents get you to sleep. So if they ever need a lullaby, they can read this to you, and I'm sure it will do the trick.

We are about to celebrate the High Holidays. In a few years, you'll know that these days mark our new year, a time to think about the past and the future. For me, after seeing you, it is a very special new year. I don't feel old; I feel younger than ever. Just as we all feel reborn and renewed on Rosh Hashanah, I feel reborn because of your birth and renewed through the sight of brand new life.

I'm not sure that I know what life is all about, but maybe, life is about itself. My father, your great-grandfather, is a wise rabbi, and he says that before anything else life is about the perpetuation of life. So maybe you are the answer to all of the questions.

So what is it that I want to say to you, first grandchild; first child of my first child? I want to say so many things. I want to tell you about the world you've just been born into, about your place in this world, about who you were, who you are, and who I hope you'll become.

I'll begin as you'll begin, with faces. You already have some sense of your mother's face and your father's face. They are your world right now. They give you everything that you need. You know their voices. And in a way, faces and voices will be the story of the first part of your life. You will look at those faces and see love. And you will hear love in their voices.

But the whole world is not made up of loving, smiling faces and comforting, soft voices. So I'm going to give you the bad news and I'm going to tell you the truth and you're not going to like it which is okay because I don't like it either. There are bad people, evil people in this world. There are no monsters, no *boogeymen*, no wicked witches like the ones in your fairy tales, but there are people who act like monsters and are as scary as *boogeymen* and are as powerful as wicked witches. And your parents will protect you from them and you will be fine. And later, when you grow up, you will protect yourself from them.

Why are they this way? I don't know. I cannot figure out why some people want to hurt other people. One guess is that they were hurt themselves and they're taking it out on someone else. Maybe, but if someone hurt me the last thing in the world I would ever want to do would be to hurt someone else in the same way. So I don't know why they want to hurt. But I do know that this world is full of problems because of these bad people and the fact that good people are forced to fight them. If we ever lose some battles against them, don't be afraid, because we will win in the end.

How do I know that good people will win? Because God did not create this world so that it would destroy itself. God is on the side of truth and good. And you live in a country that fights for the good.

That brings me to two big subjects, God and your country.

When you'll first think about God, you will see a face and maybe even hear a voice. And later you'll ask why you can't see God. Well, you can't see love, right? You see *expressions* of your parents' love, you see it in their faces and you hear it in their voices. But you can't see love.

In the same way, you can't see God, but you can see Him in His expressions, in the world, in the trees and the river and the sky and the sun. And you can hear His voice in the songs we sing and the prayers we say.

I'll talk about your country next. You live in a great country at a great time in history. You were born at the right time in the right place. You have no idea how lucky you are to be born now and here. Doctors will give you shots and you will cry. You will hate to go the doctor. But those shots will stop you from getting the sicknesses that used to cause children terrible problems. If you had been born at a different time in another place, you might not have lived past your first week. We take so many things for granted, but I don't want you to take anything for granted. I want you to know that you are a very lucky little boy to have been born into a family that can give you everything you need. Not all families can provide the care that we can, but we hope that in the not too distant future every baby born will have what you have and will be protected by good care as they grow up.

So you're lucky in that way, but you're also lucky to have been born in the twenty-first century in this country. You will hear people criticize this country's leaders and argue over issues but the worst leader of our country is still a good person trying to do good things and the worst argument is between two sides trying to do what is right and best. Our country makes mistakes. But when you hear people say bad things about this nation, always know that America is a great country striving to be even greater. Not everyone has the same rights. Everyone, no matter whether they're a boy or a girl, or have a different color skin, or have something that holds them back in some way from regular activity, everyone should have the same rights and opportunities. And this country is trying to make that so. We have a long way to go, but we've come a very long way. So love this country and show it: Respect the flag, pledge allegiance and sing the national anthem.

You have a special reason to appreciate this country. You are Jewish. Let me explain what that means. A long time ago, four thousand years ago, God saw that people were being cruel to each other. At an earlier point, God had flooded the world and destroyed all the bad people. He didn't want to do that again, so His next plan was to take one person who would be a teacher to all of the other people and try to get them to be good. That man's name was Abraham, and he was your great-great grandfather to the 160th great. God had a simple idea: People should be good to each other. They should not hurt each other. They should help each other.

God had another great revelation for Abraham. Before Abraham, people believed that there were many gods, and that those gods fought each other and that they couldn't control the world anyway. The world, they thought, was controlled by the Fates, and it didn't matter whether you were good or bad, the Fates decided what would happen to you and everything was decided by chance. Through Abraham, God revealed that there is one God and that He *does* care whether we are good or bad. If you believe in one God, you should be good, because that's why He made you. So the two ideas, that people should be good to each other, and that God wants us to be good, go together. These ideas are the basis of our religion, Judaism. These ideas have changed the world. They changed the world somewhat, but not enough, not yet. People still aren't good to each other.

Doesn't seem so hard, does it? Everyone should have listened, right? But 4000 years later, Abraham's great to the 160th generation grandchild, you live in a world that cannot grasp these simple rules. So we, the great-grandchildren of Abraham, still have a lot of work to do.

We Jewish people have a job, the job first done by Abraham. We were chosen to do a job and we choose to do that job, the way that your parents have jobs and the way you have a job, which right now is just to eat and sleep. We are not better than anyone else because we're Jewish. But we're certainly not worse than anyone else either. We have our jobs and they have theirs.

You'll spend many years thinking about what job you'll do, what you want to be when you grow up. You'll play trucker and fireman and you'll be many things in your imagination. Play all you want, but someday, when you decide for real, be somebody who does something for other people. Be a face that looks with goodness at other people and be a voice that says nice things to other people. That's what being Jewish means.

And that's why we're Jewish, not just because we were born into a certain family but because it is who we are in our minds and hearts, not just Jewish by birth but by spirit. And that spirit inspires, us, breathes life into us, just as God, somehow, in the greatest miracle I've ever seen, whispered a soul into a new being inside my own baby's stomach.

Judaism teaches us not to be satisfied with the world as it is, to constantly be pushing the program of Abraham.

Judaism teaches us to do what we're supposed to do even when we don't feel like it.

Judaism teaches us to tell the truth and to seek the truth. We're open. We don't say we know what we know and we are what we are and that's it.

Judaism teaches us to keep trying to be better. Every day, we keep trying to be better and help others.

You'll grow up with Judaism all around you. You'll see the candles lit on Shabbat evening and you'll love the light. Someday you'll understand that our people have been lighting those candles and singing those blessings for thousands of years. Your parents are raising you the way they were raised by their parents who were raised the same way by their parents going back as far as anyone can see. When you stare wide-eyed at those candles, you are every Jewish baby who stared the same way, loving the light, feeling the love of your parents, blessing God and cherishing the special day we call the Sabbath.

Someday, maybe, when you're much, much older and you read this letter, I won't be around. I'm working very hard to be around for a long time, but you never know what's going to be. So when that happens at some point, what you should know is that one of my greatest comforts was you, because you're my way of knowing that I'm going on in this world. And I'll be OK. Death is very scary because we don't know that much about it and it separates people who love each other. You'll have nights when you'll lie there in bed being scared of what will happen. But what we call death, which sounds so terrible and final, is really another way of being: You know everything and you are with God. It's fine, except the part that you can't be with some of the people you love.

For many years, there was always a voice in the back of my head saying:

I know what I know
We come and we go

But now, that's not the way it feels anymore. I knew my grandparents and now I know a grandchild. And I am part of a continuum, a flow, a river, and I'm standing here in the middle of the river and I'm not drowning, I can feel the water around me but I stand in my place and enjoy the flow.

You'll get tired and bored of a certain game that people play, about how you have your mother's this and your father's that. We grown-ups play that game because we desperately want to feel the connection to you, even if it's just that you have your uncle's lips.

But for all of those games, at some point you will look in a mirror and know that it's your face, and that will be quite a moment. You will see yourself as a separate person. And if, as you grow up, you see your uncle's lips or your father's eyes or your mother's hair staring back from the mirror, don't think that makes you any the less your own person. Because no person is just him or herself; we are each a product of thousands of years of learning and teaching and trying to be sane in an insane world and trying to be good in a world that laughs at goodness.

And all of those people are in you. The past flows through you in a hundred channels. Not just the parts you can see in the mirror, and not just in these mysterious things we call genes.

You're even more than all that.
You are all of their hopes.

All of those Jewish people, who were treated so badly but kept going, kept hoping, kept praying that the future would be better. And you are that future.

Day by day, you will learn about this world. I believe in an ancient idea that before you were born, an angel touched you right above the middle of your lip, making that little hollow, so that you would forget everything you knew and learn it for yourself as you grow.

I believe that learning is remembering, that as a human being and as a Jewish person you have thousands of years of memories. And that's why we learn so well, because we are remembering.

And your identity, who you are at the core of your being, is shaped by your memories.

When you'll hear the *Shema*, you will remember and when you'll see the Shabbat candles or the Hanukkah candles or hear the *Mah Nishtana* or the *Kol Nidre*, something in your Jewish soul will remember and you will respond in emotional and spiritual ways.

But not yet. Right now, you should just lie there and eat and sleep and get ready for your life. You'll need a lot of energy. You'll be going through several stages very quickly. Before you know it, you'll be cruising in the playpen. There are different stages in life. You're in one stage and I'm in another. The trick is to enjoy each stage for what it is. I'm not jealous of your parents for getting to wake up every night and take care of you. Been there, done that. In fact, right now, I'm not jealous of anyone, because I got to see you. Enjoy each stage. Don't rush.

I know that you agree: You just want to eat your pacifier. You just want someone to give you what you want when you want it.

And if you're like some people, you'll never get beyond this stage. You'll smoke a cigarette instead of eating a rattle and you'll demand that everyone give you what you want when you want it.

But I pray that you won't be like that. I pray that you will be someone who cares about other people.

So enjoy yourself now, because I expect you to grow up into someone who gives to others. Eat that pacifier and scream your little heart out because it won't be long before you're going to have to give back.

So that's my letter to you on the day when you become part of our covenant with God and right before your first High Holidays, little grandson. Love your parents, thank God, cherish your country, and know who you are: You are the 160th generation great-grandchild of Abraham. He started a people and a religion that, for four thousand years, has, generation by generation, person by person, worked to make a better world.

Eat your pacifier now. Because very soon, *boychick*, it's going to be your turn.